M000231233

AFFECTIVE SELF-ESTEEM

Lesson Plans for Affective Education

Katherine Krefft, M.Ed., Ph.D.

Accelerated Development Inc.
Publishers
Muncie   Indiana

AFFECTIVE SELF-ESTEEM

Lesson Plans for Affective Education

© Copyright 1993 by Accelerated Development Inc.

10 9 8 7 6 5 4 3 2 1

Printed in the United States of America

All rights reserved. No part of this book may be reproduced or transmitted in any form or means, electronic or mechanical, including photocopying, recording, or by an informational storage and retrieval system, without permission in writing from Accelerated Development Inc. Permission is granted to reproduce "Activity Sheets" for classroom use only, not for resale.

Technical Development: Tanya Benn
Cynthia Long
Marguerite Mader
Shaeney Pigman
Sheila Sheward

Library of Congress Cataloging-in-Publication Data

Krefft, Katherine, 1946-
    Affective self-esteem : lesson plans for affective education / Katherine Krefft.
        p.   cm.
    Includes bibliographical references.
    ISBN 1-55959-048-3   (pbk.)
     1. Affective education--United States.   2. Curriculum planning--United States.   3. Self-esteem in adolescence--United States.
I. Title.
LB1072.K74 1993
371.1'02--dc20

                                92-55064
                                   CIP

LCN: 92-55064

ISBN: 1-55959-048-3

Order additional copies from:

ACCELERATED DEVELOPMENT INC., PUBLISHERS
3808 West Kilgore Avenue, Muncie, Indiana 47304-4896
Toll Free Order Number 1-800-222-1166

To Jack and Bob Kennedy
Who led us to believe
Camelot is possible.

PREFACE

"JUST SAY NO" IS NOT ENOUGH

The rate of suicide among teenagers has doubled since 1970. About 30% of youngsters have tried drugs or alcohol. Among older teens 50% have used drugs. One in four youngsters live in single parent homes. The leading cause of death for teens is the fatalities from alcohol related accidents. Is this America in the golden age of modernism?

Both the suicide that is instantly lethal and the slow suicide of long-term substance abuse are symptoms of a sick society. Were the illness due to lack of intelligence, we would have cured it decades ago. The heart, our human emotions, is the key to the solution, not the intellect.

Drug abuse is an intergenerational emotional cycle in which parental abuse of drugs, primarily alcohol and nicotine, models substance abuse for the next generation. "Just say no" is not enough because our emotions continue to exist no matter how many decades we say no to them.

A NEW STRATEGY

What does one do after saying no? Knowing what not to do is one thing. Knowing *what* to do is quite another. To win the War on Drugs, we need more than slogans. We need strategies. AFFECTIVE SELF-ESTEEM is a strategy for teaching the what-to-do.

Drug use, suicide, and other unacceptable social behavior are all ways of responding to uncomfortable emotions. Drug use, in particular, involves the ***alteration of the biochemistry of emotion.*** A valid strategy for addressing substance abuse must involve incorporating knowledge of the physiology of emotion into practical strategies for constructive emotional expression.

AFFECTIVE EDUCATION DEFINED

Psychologists and educators have long debated how we may make our educational system more **ef**fective. But can effective education exist without **af**fective education? What good is reading, writing, and arithmetic to a youngster dead from a drug overdose or suicide?

Affective education is systematic instruction about the nature of emotions and how to constructively manage them. It is not therapy. It is not counseling.

If the lessons raise issues, as they may, that are highly charged and painful, referral to a psychologist is the responsible course of action. However, as learners discover how to effectively and responsibly handle their emotions, beneficial therapeutic outcomes will become evident.

WHO MAY USE AFFECTIVE SELF-ESTEEM

We may not all be students, but we are all learning. Students are found only in formal educational institutions, but learners are everywhere. Thus, in AFFECTIVE SELF-ESTEEM the word, learner, is substituted for the word, student. Though designed to be taught in educational settings such as high schools, these lesson plans are suitable for adolescents of all ages who hunger for new knowledge about constructive emotional expression.

With adaptation AFFECTIVE SELF-ESTEEM may be useful in prisons, residential treatment and foster homes, and substance abuse treatment programs. The material may prove a valuable adjunct to twelve-step groups, for work with the battered and abused, perpetrators as well, and for educators who teach parenting. The content of these lessons would constitute useful in-service education for therapists, educators, and the helping professions in general.

EMOTIONS: THE MAGIC WELLSPRING

As we see in Lesson One, the transforming power of emotions is pure wizardry. Emotions deluge, cascade, stream, saturate, gush, swirl, and pour in and through us like a magic spring of living water. We may drown in fear, soak and steam in anger, be submerged in grief, or be engulfed in guilt. *Or,* we may claim possession of the magic wand of enchantment by learning to convert fear to courage, anger to determination, grief to empathy, and guilt to new resolve.

By examining our challenging emotions, we are able to release our fear of them. No cognitive approach can remove pain from uncomfortable emotions. But with knowledge we may learn to go with the flow and keep our heads above water.

EMOTIONS AND SELF-ESTEEM

"Build self-esteem" is often advocated as the way to "fix" high risk and substance abusing youngsters. Too often self-esteem building programs fail to directly teach about emotions. But self-esteem cannot exist without constructive emotional expression.

As we experience ourselves as competent to survive amidst challenging emotions, self-respect grows. Conversely, when we interpret fear as a sign we are "wimpy fraidy-cats," self-esteem plummets. When we find we have acted destructively out of anger, feelings may deteriorate even to self-hatred. But when we effectively channel anger into determination, self-respect rises.

Self-esteem begins with the validation of emotions. When we raise youngsters with "Don't be afraid," "Don't get mad," and "Don't cry" directives, we are raising citizens with a "Don't feel" command well embedded. So, when we then turn within only to find a muddle of emotions, "Don't feel" quickly translates to "Don't be." Reason and intelligence may know better, but the feeling heart whispers, *"If my feelings are no good, I am no good."* Affective education **necessarily** builds self-esteem.

THE A, B, C's

The strategies for action taught in AFFECTIVE SELF-ESTEEM are concrete, simple, and pragmatic. When one is highly emotional, a detailed plan will not be remembered. An *affective* strategy like an anger management plan must be clear, practical, and routine to the point of being automatic. Thus, the A, B, C's consist of three steps: (A) Allow the emotion, (B) Be with the emotion, and (C) Channel the emotion.

From the time they are taught in Lesson Three the A, B, C's should be repeatedly listed and reinforced. The excitements of everyday life provide generous opportunities for teachers and counselors to advise, *"Stop! Let's apply the A, B, C's to this."* Practical application is always a key to learning. Instruction about emotions is no exception.

INTRODUCTION

In research at Rutgers University Dr. Robert J. Pandina has elucidated the role of emotions in substance abuse and other unacceptable behaviors. According to his research, youngsters who are highly reactive, impulsive, and prone to intense, long-term uncomfortable emotions are most at risk for substance abuse. Drug use, an attempt to relieve the pain of strong feelings, further decreases an already low level of personal competence.

Significantly, Dr. Pandina's research[1] has found that drug abusers are profoundly challenged by uncomfortable emotions and lack of competency *before* they start drug use. From his research Dr. Pandina has concluded that addressing affect issues is more powerful remediation than proclaiming the dangers of drugs. *"Learning and instructing in the management of affectivity may prove to be a key and a major challenge to management of drug abuse and dependency,"* Dr. Pandina has stated.

THE PLAN OF AFFECTIVE SELF-ESTEEM

The composition of the lesson plans offers flexibility to suit the needs of particular groups of learners. By design the activities are interdisciplinary and adaptable. The teacher's judgment is crucial to modifying both content and sequence of the lessons. Thus, space is provided for recording the teacher's notes in the ample margins.

The first four lessons which cover the fundamentals should be taught initially. After this the teacher may take the lessons in the order presented. But each of the series of lessons on anger, fear, and grief, and the single lesson on guilt are separate units. Any unit may be taught next after the four introductory lessons. However, revising the sequence of the content may require alterations in the suggested activities.

COMPONENTS

Each lesson is composed of five sections: (1) Objectives, (2) Materials, (3) Content, (4) Activities, and (5) Bulletin Boards.

---

[1] Adler, T. (1990, January). Some negative feelings can fuel abuse of drugs. *APA Monitor* (pp. 6-7).

Section 1 frames two or three behavioral objectives. These goals are concrete and tied to practical activities and projects that are necessary to retention of content. Section 2 lists necessary materials which include items such as notebooks for journals.

Having learners keep a journal is strongly recommended. Writing about feelings is an excellent technique for clarifying and getting a grip on emotions. The process of writing requires the application of the Magic A, B, C's since the writer must ask "What do I feel? How does it feel *to me*?" The act of writing enables the learner to perform Step C, constructive expression of emotion.

The largest division of the lesson is Section 3, Content. It begins with a review of the last lesson and is divided into several segments in order that the teacher may tailor material to the time limits available. A lesson may be taught in one to two fifty minute periods, in two to four twenty-five minute periods, or in smaller units such as ten minutes a day. The teacher may find the margins convenient for bracketing out the portion of material to be taught in each session.

The final major area is Section 4, Activities. These exercises are the heart of the lesson. Content is not learned until it is applied. One or more of the exercises are to be done during class, if time allows. One or more are to be assigned as "carryover" activities. The carryover may be to home as a homework assignment or to some collateral class period. The teacher must decide how to split class time between participatory activities and presentation of knowledge.

Each lesson ends with Section 5, Bulletin Boards. The suggested material is meant for more than classroom decoration. Prominent displays of helpful words provide aids for times of stress. When highly charged with emotions, the mind needs a short, simple directive that is easily repeated over and over. Learning how to manage emotions is in great part learning how to "Give yourself a good talking to."

INTERDISCIPLINARY DESIGN OF
AFFECTIVE SELF-ESTEEM

Emotions are an intrinsic part of life. We try to parcel them out, pigeonhole or segment them, and wall them off from what we label reason and duty. We fail. Whatever we do, wherever we go, we take our emotions with us. Studying emotions in the abstract is unwise. Doing so, we would learn everything about emotions but nothing about ourselves.

TEACHING OPTIONS

Therefore, AFFECTIVE SELF-ESTEEM encourages a strongly interdisciplinary approach which allows several teaching options. A special time period may be devoted to the core curriculum. The material may be made part of a school health curriculum. Indeed, there is rationale for placing some lessons in science class, too. Existing curricula for the biological sciences and health teach the nature of the nervous system and endocrine system but not what to do when your racing hormones have you so nervous you could scream.

Social studies, language arts, and art provide enormous opportunities for exploring and expressing emotions. Since Socrates and Aristotle, we have liked to pretend that reason drives the course of nations, at least of *our* nation whichever one that happens to be. History itself reveals the ugly truth. Prejudice is a distortion of fear. War is a distortion of anger. Rage, terror, grief, and guilt drive nations no less than individuals.

Language arts and art also provide natural means for integrating AFFECTIVE SELF-ESTEEM into the curricula. Literature and all forms of artistic presentation are the primary, civilized modes of constructive emotional expression. Fighting is unacceptable. Screaming is frowned upon. How then are we to relieve ourselves of passionate emotion?

Tempestuous poetry, creative writing, powerful art, ecstatic and fiery music are the necessary refinements of civilization because without them we have no safety valves for intense emotion. Help each learner find one, just one, modality into which the depths of emotion may pour, and you have succeeded in accomplishing the purpose of AFFECTIVE SELF-ESTEEM.

TEACHING THE LESSONS

As Dorothy commented on her own magical journey to Oz, *"It is usually best to begin at the beginning."* Carefully reading through all the lessons is essential. Pay particular attention to content that strikes you in an unusually forceful way. Most who will teach these lessons received no analogous instruction in childhood. But we all learned about emotions. That learning consisted of the absorption of common myths and misunderstandings. With that learning came huge voids we struggled to fill from harsh experience.

HONESTY AND HUMILITY

Possibly, then, you may find herein facts that yield insight into your own emotions. This is normal. To expect yourself to know what you were never taught would be unfair. Teaching these lessons requires the humility to thoroughly examine your beliefs about emotions. It requires the honesty to openly assess your own management of uncomfortable emotions.

Humility and honesty are the only ways to assure that your blind spots will not subtly color what you teach. In order not to pass on misunderstandings about emotions, honestly pinpointing those misunderstandings is an absolute prerequisite.

In settings where more than one instructor will be involved, a joint planning group is suggested to provide a forum for sharing personal feelings and questions raised by the impact of these lessons. If a particular segment of the content has a more personal meaning for you, *"Talk it out."*

YOU ARE THE MODEL

Determine to share your emotions with learners. No other teaching technique is as powerful as modeling. *"Do what I say, not what I do"* only alienates learners. Modeling conveys permission. Our society is so stunted emotionally that even with lessons of applicable information youngsters will shy away from constructive emotional expression. Knowledge is not enough. Learners must believe that practicing the application of that knowledge in your presence is *okay*. You, the teacher, are the one to nurture that permission week after week.

THE POWER OF WORDS

In AFFECTIVE SELF-ESTEEM the words positive and negative are generally avoided as descriptors of emotions. Instead, comfortable emotions such as love, joy, and surprise are contrasted with the uncomfortable, challenging ones of anger, fear, grief, and guilt. We may think of anger and fear as negative, but such a label masks their inherent potential for good. Emotions are neither good nor bad, positive nor negative. They just are.

Similarly, we refrain from using the popular phrase, "coping with emotions." To cope is to endure and contend with. Coping carries the connotation of fighting, of a hard struggle for survival. *"Cope with it!"* implies *"Put up with the pain."* A more advantageous approach is to think and speak in terms of constructive management of emotions. "Handle it!" bears the subtle message, *"I know you **can** handle it."*

Learners must see *you* using the knowledge contained in AFFECTIVE SELF-ESTEEM. Education about emotions is more than a set of lesson plans. Affective education is a way of thinking that incorporates appropriate emotional expression into everyday life. Such new learning reveals itself in the very language we use.

OLD LANGUAGE	NEW LANGUAGE
• For the third time, be quiet!	I feel angry when I have to ask you three times to be quiet.
• Stop that! Someone might get hurt.	It scares me to see you roughhousing because I've seen youngsters get hurt like that.
• Can't you *ever* follow the rules? You're punished!	You know the rules. I feel angry when you don't follow them. Maybe you're angry, too. Let's talk about it.
• What's the matter with you? We spent three classes on this! You all have extra homework tonight.	Now, class, I thought we worked so hard on this. I feel sad that so many of you still have not got it. Help me figure out a way to teach it so everyone is able to get it.
• Who do you think you are treat someone like that?	I feel angry when I see you treat someone so unfairly.
• You guys let me down. I *told* you to study.	I'm really disappointed with how the class did on the test.
• Read your books. (Silence)	We're going to do some quiet work today. As you know, my father's funeral was yesterday and, frankly, I'm feeling sad and out of energy just now.

To say, *"Class, I'm thrilled you did so well!"* is easy. To be honest about one's uncomfortable emotions is enormously more challenging. **Accepting** that challenge is the heart of AFFECTIVE SELF-ESTEEM. In affective education the **teacher** allows, admits, feels, and expresses emotions. Model what you teach.

HUMOR

Another key is the generous exercise of humor. The tragedy of teen suicide and the horror of a drug epidemic so vast that we must conceptualize the cure as a "war" easily blind us to the joy and mystery of emotions. In our world life is frightening enough. To paraphrase Lincoln, all people are afraid of most things some of the time.

But we terrify ourselves literally to death by our **fear of the pain** of uncomfortable emotions. Fear is uncomfortable, not tormenting. Anger is troublesome and painful but yet not impossible to handle. Grief is anguish, not torture. Guilt is no fun, but it does not have to be self-persecution.

The terror of emotions is self-inflicted. If our guardian angels videotaped our emotional ravings and left the tape on our doorsteps each morning, we would have no time to cringe and roar and moan and blame. We'd be too busy laughing.

WINNING THE WAR ON DRUGS

A winning strategy does not have to be complex or ornate. World War II in Europe was won by the consistent application of a simple strategy. Invade and advance mile by mile all the way to Berlin. Ike's plan had less frills than his uniform. The only difference from one mile to the next was that some were more bloody, some less so.

No reason was an acceptable excuse for stopping the advance. Being surrounded on all sides was no excuse. In 1944 General Anthony McAuliff and the 101st Airborne were surrounded at Bastogne. The Nazi commander sent an invitation to surrender. McAuliff, anticipating ultimate victory, sent back a one word reply, *"Nuts."* If America is to win the War on Drugs, it shall take just such persistent determination and fierce resolve. A touch of wry humor would help, too.

CONTENTS

LIST OF ACTIVITY SHEETS

We all do no end of feeling, and we mistake it for thinking.

Mark Twain

Twain, M. (1935). "Corn-Pone Opinions" *The family Mark Twain* (p. 1403). New York: Harper & Brothers.

UNIT I:
EMOTIONS

OUR MAGIC WAND

OBJECTIVES

Learners will demonstrate their comprehension of

1. basic definitions as demonstrated by using the dictionary and their own words to define key terms,

2. reasons for studying emotions and how emotions are like magic as shown by discussion in class and by sharing personal feedback on emotions, and

3. the nature of common myths and misunderstandings about emotions as shown by discussion in class and by making journal entries.

MATERIALS

- Magic Wand

- Chalkboard or overhead projector

- Dictionaries, one for each learner

- Journals for learners

- Activity Sheets 1.1, "Knowing My Emotions" and 1.2, "I'm Bad, I'm Bad, I'm Really Bad"

CONTENT

1. **Why We Need to Study Emotions**

   Introduce the subject to learners by asking, *"What reasons can you think of for studying about our emotions?"* List responses on the board. Continue with, *"What emotions do **you** want to learn more about?"*

2. **Feelings or Facts?**

   Introduce the subject to learners by asking, *"What is a **feeling**? What is a **fact**? What is an **emotion**?"*

Accept spontaneous answers. Then have learners look those words up in the dictionary. Write answers and words in bold face (as shown below) on the board.

Feeling	Emotion	Fact

3. **Emotions versus Beliefs**

Point out that the word feeling is used loosely to indicate both emotions and beliefs. *"I feel sad"* states an emotion. *"I feel dictatorship is bad"* states a belief as does, *"I don't feel like you're listening."* Ask for other examples.

Explain that feelings explored in AFFECTIVE SELF-ESTEEM are *emotions,* not beliefs.

4. **Emotions Are Magic**

Write on the board, *Emotions are magic.* Then ask, *"Why are emotions magic? How are emotions and magic alike?"* List responses on the board. If necessary, convert the following ideas to questions in order to prompt answers.

Emotions and magic are alike because

a. both transform one thing into another;

b. both are powerful and frightening;

c. both are not always what they appear on the surface;

d. both produce effects by unseen, invisible means;

e. both give special ability to control events;

f. we have many misunderstandings about both;

g. both are mysterious, absorbing, surprising, enchanting, and puzzling; and

h. both hold our attention and never cease to amaze and fascinate us.

5. **Misunderstandings and Myths**

In the discussion some learners may give responses that are myths about emotions. Generate further comments by inquiring, *"What common misunderstandings do we have about emotions?"* Misunderstandings about emotions are legion.

a. **Emotions Are Animalistic and Degrading.**

They make us weak and uncool. Some examples of disparaging remarks that reveal these attitudes are

"Stop being so emotional";
"Don't lose your cool";
"Don't give in to your lower self";
*"You know how **she** is—so emotional";*
"He's so strong, he never shows how he feels";
"He was as mad as a bull";
"She was whimpering like a wounded animal";
"He was laughing like a hyena";
"Poor scared lamb";
"You scaredycat, you're a wimp"; and
"If I feel bad feelings, I'm bad."

b. **Emotions Are Bad Because They Are Irrational.**

Nonrational is *different,* not bad. Emotions are a necessary counterbalance to cold reason. As Pascal said, *"The heart has reasons that reason does not."* Some examples of this myth are

"I was so upset I was going crazy,"
"He's insane when he's mad,"
"I was scared out of my mind," and
"I must be stupid to let this get to me."

c. **Emotions Are Just Tools for Control.**

A favorite myth is that people who show emotions are merely manipulative. People who believe this are themselves afraid of emotion. Some examples are

"People stir up my emotions just to be mean";
"You really know how to push my buttons";
"You make me so mad";
"I can't help the way I feel";
"I need someone to make me happy";
"If I feel that way, I'll do something terrible";
"She makes me feel guilty"; and
"He scares me."

6. **The Magic Wand**

Show learners your Magic Wand. Explain, *"This is our new Magic Wand. What do magic wands do? What are they for?"* Everyone knows that magic wands change one thing into another: like Cinderella's pumpkin into a coach. The magic wand is what the American Indians call a Power Stick. All sorts of marvels are possible with such power!

Continue, *"Every Magic Wand needs a name. Let's give our wand a very special, unique name."* By this point learners should be very curious about how you intend to use the wand. Tell them they shall have to wait for the next lesson to find out.

ACTIVITIES

Choose one or a combination. Assign one for carryover.

1. **Journaling—My Challenges**

   Assign learners to answer in their journals:

   a. What emotions are my greatest challenges?

   b. What misunderstandings have I had about emotions?

   c. What myths about emotions do people in my family have?

   d. What emotions do I most prefer?

2. **Group Activity**
   "Knowing My Emotions" (Activity Sheet 1.1)

   Break students into small groups and as a group have members complete Activity Sheet 1.1, "Knowing My Emotions." Have each group elect a leader to report results back to the whole class.

3. **Individual Activity**
   "Knowing My Emotions" (Activity Sheet 1.1)

   Direct each learner to complete Activity Sheet 1.1 alone.

4. **Sleepwalking Through Life: A Fable**

   Knowing little or nothing about our emotions and about why we do what we do, many of us sleepwalk our way through life. This activity is designed to develop an awareness of why a study of AFFECTIVE SELF-ESTEEM is constructive.

   Divide the class into two groups according to sex. Instruct each group, *"Work together to invent a fable about a character who lived his or her whole life **asleep!** That's right. Every morning this person seemed to wake up, but actually the whole day was spent sleepwalking."*

   Groups work independently of each other. However, members of a group work together to compose their fables. The teacher may use this opportunity to teach about and share examples of fables as a literary form. Have one member of each group read the fable to the class. Compare and contrast the results.

5. **Once I Was Upset**

Upset describes many emotions including fear and grief. Often *"I'm upset"* is a backhanded way of saying, *"I'm angry."* Let learners discover this on their own by writing a short essay of three to four paragraphs titled, "Once I Was Upset."

Instruct learners, *"Describe a specific incident when you were upset. What did you mean when you said you were upset? What emotions were you feeling when you felt upset?"* Essays may be read aloud at the end of this class period or beginning of the next.

6. **Doing versus Being "Bad"**
   "I'm Bad, I'm Bad, I'm Really Bad" (Activity Sheet 1.2)

Assign the activity sheet titled with the name of a popular song by Michael Jackson. If possible, play the song as introduction.

Tip to the Teacher

Teenagers may want to quickly move the talk into discussion about sexual feelings. The first lesson is intended solely as an introduction to the subject of human emotions. Use your discretion in allowing the discussion to diverge and ramble. If appropriate, you may wish to point out that sexuality combines EMOTIONS such as joy and love with FEELINGS such as sexual arousal which is an array of physiological sensations, not an emotion.

BULLETIN BOARD MATERIAL

Use the bulletin board to add pictures, stories, and sayings that relate to the topic. The following are examples of sayings that could be used.

1. Feelings are neither good nor bad. They just are.

2. Emotions are our magic!

3. *The fewer the facts, the stronger the opinion.*
   Arnold Glasow

Name: _____ Date: _____

Activity Sheet 1.1
KNOWING MY EMOTIONS

Complete the following sentences. If necessary, you may continue a long sentence on the back of this sheet.

1. I feel happy when _____.

2. I feel afraid when _____.

3. I get mad at _____.

4. I feel good about _____.

5. I feel sad about _____.

6. I am surprised when _____.

7. I feel delighted when _____.

8. I feel excited about _____.

9. I feel guilty when _____.

10. I feel self-satisfaction when _____.

11. When I'm happy, I _____.

12. When I'm mad, I _____.

13. When I'm in love, I _____.

14. When I feel sad, I _____.

15. When I'm contented, I _____.

16. When I feel guilty, I _____.

17. When I'm excited and elated, I _____.

18. When I'm afraid, I _____.

19. When I'm surprised, I _____.

20. When I'm content, I _____.

21. Right now I feel _____

_____.

*Permission granted to reproduce for classroom use. Taken from **Affective Self-Esteem** by Katherine Krefft, M.Ed., Ph.D. © 1993, Accelerated Development Inc., Publishers, 3808 W. Kilgore Avenue, Muncie, IN 47304-4896.*

Name: _____   Date: _____

Activity Sheet 1.2
"I'M BAD, I'M BAD, I'M REALLY BAD"

People are NOT bad, but they sometimes do unacceptable things. Think about something you once did that later made you feel very bad about yourself. Describe what you did.

_____

_____

Now think carefully. What were you feeling BEFORE this incident occurred? Angry? Scared? Hurt? Jealous? Sad? Circle your answer and tell about any other emotion you felt.

_____

_____

What was your self-talk BEFORE the incident? The quotation marks show that the self-talk is what you say to yourself.

" _____

_____ "

Was some of your self-talk coming from a wounded ego? Hurt feelings? Or because you felt put down? If so, write the self-talk here.

" _____

_____ "

Was some of your self-talk coming from a belief that you had been treated unfairly? If so, write the self-talk here.

" _____

_____ "

What were your emotions AFTER the incident? Your self-talk?

" _____

_____ "

Think of a more constructive plan for handling the emotions and self-talk that led up to the incident. If you like, ask for input from a friend. Describe that plan here and on the back of this sheet.

*Permission granted to reproduce for classroom use. Taken from **Affective Self-Esteem** by Katherine Krefft, M.Ed., Ph.D. © 1993, Accelerated Development Inc., Publishers, 3808 W. Kilgore Avenue, Muncie, IN 47304-4896.*

THE ENCHANTED POWERHOUSE

OBJECTIVES

Learners will demonstrate their comprehension of

1. the dichotomy of reason and emotion and their different qualities and aspects as shown by discussing them and assigning them to The Head or The Heart;

2. the dichotomy of comfortable and uncomfortable emotions and the power to choose feelings as demonstrated by class discussion activities with the Magic Wand; and

3. the natural, water-like flow of emotions as shown by collecting pictures of water and telling, writing, and illustrating stories related to the pictures.

MATERIALS

- Magic Wand

- Chalkboard or overhead projector

- Images of water: magazine cut-outs or other pictures including photograph of a major dam like Hoover Dam

- Journals for learners

- Activity Sheets 2.1, "Fairy Tale of the Magic Water," and 2.2, "Our Cheating Hearts"

CONTENT

1. **Review**

   Collect carryover assignment. Review the last lesson.

   - Define these three words: feeling, emotion, fact.

   - What are we going to study in these lessons?

- How are emotions and magic alike?

- State why learning about emotions is helpful.

- What common misunderstandings do we have about emotions?

- State some common disparaging remarks about emotions.

- Emotions are a necessary counterbalance to what?

- List some disparaging remarks that show the belief that emotions are manipulative tools.

- How have you used what you have learned?

2. **The Head versus The Heart**

Begin with, *"In the last lesson we considered several misunderstandings about emotions. Today we're going to take a look at some facts about emotions. We can look at ourselves in two ways: from the head and from the heart."*

Put the following diagram on the chalkboard.

The Head	The Heart

Discuss with learners various ways we demonstrate this polarity in life and in ourselves. As you do, use your Magic Wand, a pointer or yardstick, to lightly tap or indicate the learner on whom you are calling. A completed chart may look something like the following.

The Head	The Heart
Reason	Emotions
Thinking	Feeling
Logic	Intuition
Facts	Imagination
Judgment	Inspiration
Reflecting	Sensing
Detachment	Passion
Science	Art
Mathematics	Music
Grammar	Poetry
Etc.	Etc.

Conclude by pointing out that only a combination of both The Head and The Heart in balance brings us to the fullness of our human potential. Demonstrate this graphically by erasing the center line in the chart. Then, draw circles that connect each pair of words.

3. **Comfortable and Uncomfortable Emotions**

Continue by explaining that some emotions we call **comfortable** because they feel good. Those that do not, we call **uncomfortable.** Ask, *"What are the uncomfortable emotions? What are the comfortable ones?"*

a. **Pass the Wand**

Again, use the Magic Wand to indicate on whom you are calling. Then, hand the wand to a learner who answers and passes it on to someone else to answer.

Throughout these lessons the teacher may find that a helpful procedure is to write on the chalkboard words that are in bold face in the lesson plan. Thus, as you begin the discussion, list the following headings on the board.

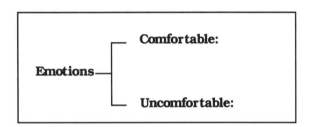

Have learners get up from their seats to fill in the chart as the wand goes around the classroom. Some comfortable emotions are **love, happiness, excitement, pride, surprise, joy, delight,** and **satisfaction.** The main uncomfortable emotions, the ones we shall study in these lessons, are **anger, fear, grief,** and **guilt.**

b. **Your Choice**

After the lists are on the board, point out to learners that they each chose whether they would list a comfortable or an uncomfortable emotion. Stress that each of us holds the same wand—has the same power—but our choices, and so our feelings, differ.

Accept all answers noncritically. One purpose of these lessons is to develop critical judgment about emotions. Learners cannot be expected to possess refined judgment about emotions after only one or two lessons.

4. **The Natural Flow of Emotions**

Explain to learners, *"One of the best ways for us to understand our emotions and how they work is to think of them like water. Let's take a look at these pictures of water. What emotions do you think of when you see each of these pictures?"*

a. **"Water, Water Everywhere"**

Show a variety of pictures of water in its many aspects: turbulent (angry), stormy (fearful, angry), empty and vast (lonely, fearful, sad, awesome), calm (peaceful), underwater depths (awesome, fearful). With each picture ask, *"Of what emotion does this picture remind you?"* Expect a wide variety of responses.

After this initial activity, explain that the natural flow of emotions is wavelike. Using a picture of gentle waves for illustration, explain, *"We experience one wave of emotion, then a lull like the trough between waves, then another wave followed by another trough. It is a process of peaks and valleys."* Emphasize to learners that to experience currents of emotion in an on-off, on-off fashion is usual and normal.

b. **Building Dams versus Going With the Flow**

But frequently we do not "go with the flow." Rather than allowing ourselves to experience the ups and downs, we build dams. Use photographs of actual dams like the Hoover Dam to make the point. Ask, *"What effect does a dam have on the flow of water?"* Continue, *"Where is the water the deepest: in front or in back of the dam? What would happen if water built up behind the dam with no release?"* As a collateral to this lesson, the scientific explanation of water pressure and hydrodynamics may be taught in science class.

Continue with, *"But what happens when a steady flow of water is channeled through the mechanisms of the dam?"* Elicit from learners the process of hydroelectricity. Elicit the understanding that a channeled flow can produce what is good and productive: electricity, the power to make things happen. But too much *undirected* water in one place at one time is destructive: a flood.

Conclude with, *"It's the same with emotions. When we let them build and build with no release, they flood out suddenly. That makes us feel out of control. But when we go with the flow and allow ourselves to feel the feeling wave by wave, we may direct and channel them ourselves. We feel in control.*

"The reservoir of emotions is our 'Enchanted Powerhouse' that makes life electric. Emotions are the electricity that motivate us to get things done. Emotions are the currents that make life exciting instead of boring."

c. **Personal Examples**

Pass the wand as you ask for examples. *"Tell me about a time you let your emotions build up until they erupted like a flood."* If learners shy away from answering, depersonalize the query, *"Let's talk about someone—no one in this room, of course—who let emotions build up to a flood."* Examples of anger will be easy, but lead learners to understand that fear, grief and even guilt may be buried and ignored until they burst out in an overwhelming flood.

Continue, *"And what did you do then? Did you get drunk? Or high? How did that change what you had been feeling? But how did you feel when you sobered up?"* Ordinarily, we dam up only uncomfortable emotions. Since comfortable emotions like joy and love are pleasant, we readily express them. We reject uncomfortable emotions because they are hard, painful, and challenging—a process of pain avoidance. Thus, another term for uncomfortable emotions is ***challenging emotions.*** Explain to learners that to push away uncomfortable emotions is not "bad." It's only human.

ACTIVITIES

Choose one or a combination. Assign one for carryover.

1. **The Quest for Your Magic Water**

    Direct learners to search for their own unique picture of Magic Water, a photograph or drawing of a scene of water that has special, personal appeal. Instruct learners, *"You are not going to choose the picture. The picture is going to choose you! For this to happen you must LISTEN with your magic inner ear for the picture that whispers, 'Take me. I'm the one. I'm your picture of Magic Water.'"*

    Give learners a menu of items they may do:

    a. Frame the picture. Draw or construct a special, "magic" frame for the picture.

    b. Write a dialogue with the water speaking in first person and the writer speaking in third person. The story might begin, *"I am Water. I am magic for [name of learner] because . . ."* Explain to learners that an important point is to have Water and learner speak.

        Suggest that the learner take the name Seeker and ask questions like, *"Water, why am I so sad so often? What do I do when I feel like a hurricane? Will my little boat sink in the storm?"* Elicit similar questions from the group before each individual begins to write.

    c. Draw or paint the picture. Post artwork that illustrates stories and dialogues.

    d. Trade pictures. As one learner holds another's picture, each learner may tell how that picture is like its owner, or alternately may tell the learner's own personal associations and impressions of the picture.

2. **Journaling—The Tale of the Time of the Flood**

Instruct learners to write in their journals a short "Tale of the Time of the Flood." The tale tells of someone known to the learner who let emotions build up until they flooded out in a torrent. Learners may use substitute, made-up names. List the four uncomfortable emotions (**anger, fear, grief, guilt**) on the board as you give the assignment. Explain that learners should clearly identify the emotion or emotions that caused the flood. Tales may be shared in class.

3. **Group Activity**
"Fairy Tale of the Magic Water" (Activity Sheet 2.1)

Use the collection of pictures of water to have the learners as a group compose a "Fairy Tale of the Magic Water" (Activity Sheet 2.1). The tale may be told orally and/or written like a book with a short paragraph accompanying each illustration. Explain to learners that the narrative should relate feelings to the movement of the water. In the fairy tale water may be like a magic mirror. For example, *"When the prince became angry, the waves pounded the boat."*

Like all fairy tales this one begins, *"Once upon a time there was a _____ of Magic Water."* Using the illustrations, learners decide which of the following words or synonyms fills in the blank: ocean, lake, pond, river, brook, creek, stream, pool, lagoon, drop, dribble, trickle, drip, torrent, wave, current, flood, bead, teardrop, etc.

First, write these choices and learners' ideas on the board. Then, add names of the major characters: prince, princess, witches, wizards, and so on. As learners compose the story, the teacher is to repeatedly ask, *"What was the character feeling at that point? How did the water reflect that emotion?"*

4. **Individual Activity**
"Fairy Tale of the Magic Water" (Activity Sheet 2.1)

Assign Activity Sheet 2.1, "Fairy Tale of the Magic Water," to be completed by individuals after group activity 3, above.

5. **The Head versus the Heart Artwork**

Learners who enjoy artwork may either alone or in groups of three or four design and craft posters or displays illustrating the difference between The Head and The Heart. A large heart may represent The Heart while a profile or outline of a head may represent The Head. List the appropriate qualities on each.

6. **"Our Cheating Hearts"**
   (Activity Sheet 2.2)

   Assign the activity sheet. Divide into small groups so that learners may share feedback.

The Magic Wand

Explain to learners that throughout these lessons, we shall use the wand to indicate who has the "magic power" to speak and act in the classroom. When the teacher holds the wand, the teacher is in charge. But when a learner holds it, authority has moved to that learner. The wand is a real, tangible symbol for the fact that we each possess sole authority over our thoughts, feelings, and actions.

BULLETIN BOARD MATERIAL

1. *The heart has reasons that reason does not.*
                                        Pascal

2. Go with the flow!

Name: _____   Date: _____

Activity Sheet 2.1
FAIRY TALE OF THE MAGIC WATER

Write a fairy tale about Magic Water. These questions may help.

- What kind of Magic Water is it? Where is it?

- Why is it magic? Who uses its magic?

- What does Magic Water look like? Sound like?

- How does it feel? Does it have a taste, texture or smell?

- How is it used? Who made it into Magic Water?

- Why is it important? Why is it important **to you?**

You do not **have** to use these questions, but you may if you like.

Once upon a time there was a _____ of Magic Water. _____

_____

_____

_____

_____

_____

_____

_____

_____

_____

_____

_____

_____

_____

_____

_____

_____

Permission granted to reproduce for classroom use. Taken from **Affective Self-Esteem** *by Katherine Krefft, M.Ed., Ph.D.*
© 1993, Accelerated Development Inc., Publishers, 3808 W. Kilgore Avenue, Muncie, IN 47304-4896.

Name: _____   Date: _____

Activity Sheet 2.2
OUR CHEATING HEARTS

We lie, cheat, and steal for many reasons. But often we use dishonesty as a way to express a strong emotion. Complete this sheet with ruthless inner honesty!

1. Tell about a time you were afraid and lied.

   _____

   _____

2. Tell about a time you were mad and lied or stole.

   _____

   _____

3. Tell about a time you were afraid or mad and cheated.

   _____

   _____

4. Tell about a time you were sad or despondent and lied or stole.

   _____

   _____

5. Tell about a time you felt guilty and lied.

   _____

   _____

6. Tell about a time your feelings were hurt and you did something that later made you ashamed.

   _____

   _____

   NOTE: Face your feelings. Then, the impulse to lie, cheat, or steal will not be as strong as it was before.

*Permission granted to reproduce for classroom use. Taken from **Affective Self-Esteem** by Katherine Krefft, M.Ed., Ph.D. © 1993, Accelerated Development Inc., Publishers, 3808 W. Kilgore Avenue, Muncie, IN 47304-4896.*

MAGIC A, B, C's

OBJECTIVES

Learners will demonstrate their comprehension of

1. the A, B, C's of constructive emotional expression as manifested by discussing and listing the meaning of each step; and

2. the verbal and nonverbal channeling of emotions as shown by telling and writing stories and drawing or painting pictures about their emotions.

MATERIALS

*   Magic Wand

*   Chalkboard or overhead projector

*   A, B, C poster or display

*   Crayons or paints or colored markers and paper

*   A selection of the world's greatest literature

*   Journals for learners

*   Activity Sheets 3.1, "Applying the A, B, C's," and 3.2, "Self-talk Analysis for Upsets"

CONTENTS

1. **Review**

    Collect carryover assignment. Review the last lesson.

    *   What image best describes what emotions are like?

    *   List the differences between The Head and The Heart.

    *   Describe the natural flow of emotions.

- What happens when you do not go with the flow?

- What does a regulated, channeled flow produce?

- What is the Magic Powerhouse?

- Why do we push away uncomfortable emotions?

- What emotion do *you* have to watch so it does not build up into a flood?

- Who is in charge of you: your Head or your Heart?

- How have you used what you have learned?

- Close your eyes. What is on the bulletin board?

2. **The Magic A, B, C's of Emotions**

The A, B, C's are

A. *ALLOW.*

B. *BE WITH.*

C. *CHANNEL.*

Write the A, B, C's on the board or put up a poster with the words. Discuss each step with learners. As you lead the discussion, use the Magic Wand to select learners for giving their input.

ALLOW

To allow an emotion is to honestly recognize it for what it is. To allow is to **take ownership** for one's own emotions. It is to forthrightly label the emotion instead of pretending it is something else. It is to **identify** the emotion. To allow is to "Let it be."

Most especially, allowing is distinguishing which of the four uncomfortable emotions is being felt during times of stress. **Stress** is one of many modern concepts invented to detour us from acknowledging what we are feeling. Even stress management classes often switch participants from the actual feeling experience to the process of thinking about feeling matters without naming the emotions.

Stress is the physical and mental tension created by uncomfortable emotions. Anger and fear are usually the chief culprits. Stress, sometimes called pressure, is often thought of as something "out there" that we must "deal with." In reality, our emotional response to the "out there" is the true challenge. Thus, the Magic A, B, C's are a stress management plan that gets to and stays with the root of stress, emotions.

BE WITH

To be with an emotion is to experience it, to feel it. To be with is to encounter and, if necessary, endure the emotion: to **face it bravely** instead of running away.

Being with an emotion has a **thinking part** as well. The cognitive component is to actively practice self-talk like, *"I'll be okay. I'm just feeling strong emotion. I can take it. I'm going to find someone with whom I can talk this out."* When such self-talk is not used, the inner voice may wail, *"I'm dying. I'm going crazy. I can't take this."* Hostile, unacceptable behaviors frequently follow. (See next lesson for more on self-talk.)

Remind learners that although emotions are like water, they are a special, magical water that does not evaporate. Ignoring the emotion only adds to the water behind the dam. Ignoring emotions leads to emotions **coming out sideways,** that is, to **displacement.** The classic example is the man who is mad at his boss and so comes home and kicks the dog. Ask learners for their own examples.

CHANNEL

To channel an emotion is to **express** it, to act on it constructively. To constructively channel emotion is to express it directly. It is to feel honestly and **share** the emotion but not in a way that is harmful to self or others.

Destructive expressions of emotion are not acceptable. Elicit from learners a brief list of the myriad unacceptable ways we express emotions. Anyone may choose to act out emotions negatively.

Common expressions continue to deceive us. We act in anger and cry, *"I lost my temper."* Untrue. You did not lose your temper. You **gave** it away. *"Something came over me, and I lost control."* Untrue. You felt an emotion and chose not to **take** control. Emotions may influence our choices, but they do not rob us of the power to choose.

Continue by explaining that mature channeling of emotion falls into two broad categories, **verbal** and **nonverbal.** Add to the chart or post the following.

A. ALLOW
B. BE WITH
C. CHANNEL
    1. Verbally
    2. Non-verbally

VERBAL

The chief verbal way to channel emotions is **Talk It Out.** The very act of talking about what one is feeling uses up some of the energy of the emotion. Talking it out is not just ordinary talking. It is a process of feeling the emotion and affectively expressing it with words.

Verbally sharing an emotion often relieves the emotion even as it builds *friendship.* A friend is a person with whom one shares honest feelings. Teens are intensely interested in making and having friends. Explain that learning how to verbally channel emotions is a key step in friendship building. Disclosure about emotions is the glue that builds the bond of intimacy.

Writing about emotions is another form of verbal expression. If you have not already introduced the idea of journal keeping, this would be a good place to do so. Explain to learners that writing about feelings is one of the most constructive ways to express them. Not only is the emotion expressed, but one may discover unexpected talent in creative writing.

NONVERBAL

Constructive nonverbal expression has three key forms: crying, art and music, and physical exercise or action. Involve learners in a wide-ranging discussion of what they see as beneficial and helpful means of expressing emotions, other than talking them out. Accept all appropriate input and list suggestions on the board.

Tears

Crying is necessary and normal. It is Nature's release for men as well as women. Remind learners that men as well as women have tear ducts. Constructive crying is important as Nature's primary physiological expression of emotions: anger, fear, grief, even joy and surprise. For more on crying see Chapter 14.

Using the wand to select learners, elicit their input on the purpose and benefits of crying.

Art and Music

The world's greatest artistic expressions communicate powerful emotion. Ask for examples from art and music—classic as well as contemporary. If copies of great paintings are available, hold them up one by one as learners write or call out the emotions the painting suggests. A similar exercise may be followed with passages of great music. Alternately, the school art and music teachers may complete this portion of the lesson.

Physical Exercise or Action

Finally, emotions are physiological (in the body) and so, many times, only physical exercise or appropriate action may relieve the emotion. Under stress the immune system releases chemical messengers which stimulate the hypothalamus to release additional chemicals. These then stimulate first the pituitary and next the adrenal glands.

The result is a host of physiological changes including altered heart rate, blood pressure, and breathing pattern. When you have "butterflies in the stomach" due to fear, it is not "all in your mind." It is, in equal part, also in your body. A future lesson explores how various sports correlate with how emotions are felt in the body.

ACTIVITIES

Choose one or a combination. Assign one for carryover.

1. **Journaling—My Story**

    Put the following titles on the board. Assign learners to tell or write a story with one of these titles. Stories may be written in journals.

    A Day I Felt Very Sad

    The Maddest I Ever Got

    Once I Was Afraid

    Sometimes I Feel Guilty

    I Cry Because

    Something Sad Happened

    I Get Mad When

    Me and My Worries

2. **"Applying the A, B, C's"**
   (Activity Sheet 3.1)

    Assign the exercise. Giving examples, explain the meaning of metaphor and simile. Results may be shared in small groups or with the entire class. This sheet may be used again and again throughout the course of the lessons.

3. **"Self-talk Analysis for Upsets"**
   (Activity Sheet 3.2)

    This exercise is designed to give learners practice in identifying the overt or hidden self-talk that precipitates emotional states. As with Activity Sheet 3.1, this sheet may be used again and again, especially for real-life challenges.

Stress that quotation marks must be used to make it clear that self-talk is the actual words used. For example, learners should not write, *"It was a situation that was unfair,"* but *"This is unfair! I always get the raw end of the deal. No one cares how I feel."* A statement of apparent fact is already removed from emotion. But the word for word self-talk makes the emotion evident.

Step 4 on Activity Sheet 3.2 is crucial to learning. Often a helpful procedure is to have learners work together on constructive alternatives. Step 4 may be continued on the reverse side of the sheet.

4. Our Story

Break learners into small groups of three or four. Each group makes up one story as in Activity 1. Learners illustrate the story in booklet or storyboard format. As an added challenge, invite learners to relate the story in pictures only. The remainder of the class tells the story in words as the pictures are held up one by one.

5. Uncomfortable Emotions in Great Literature

Instruct learners, *"Find and read a story, either a novel or a short story, from the world's great literature that is mostly about one or more of the following: anger, fear, grief, or guilt. Write a book report that shows how the story is about that emotion."*

Alternately, the teacher may assign a specific story with the instructions, *"Tell what emotions this story is about. What character felt which emotion when?"*

Stories of prejudice are about fear projected outward in anger onto another. Jealousy, a popular theme of novels, is fear of loss.

The teacher may work with the language arts teacher to repeat this activity several times throughout the school year. Similarly, the "Applying the A, B, C's" exercise may be used to elucidate literary plots and characters. The A, B, C's provide a fascinating format for assessing the overt and hidden motivations of the likes of Captain Ahab.

A Word of Caution

By their nature these exercises may elicit sensitive revelations. As learners begin to trust that it is safe to talk about their emotions, personal and painful material may be shared. The teacher must be aware of the impact of these lessons and refer learners to the school psychologist, social worker, or counselor as appropriate.

BULLETIN BOARD MATERIAL

1. Talk it out!

2. A, B, C's to remember

       A. Allow.

       B. Be with.

       C. Channel.

3. *A man cannot be comfortable without his own approval.*

                     Mark Twain

Name: _____ Date: _____

Activity Sheet 3.1
APPLYING THE A, B, C'S

Describe the last time you were emotional. What happened? Who did what? Who said what?

_____

_____

AAAAAAAAAAAAAAAAA   **ALLOW**   **AAAAAAAAAAAAAAAAA**

Allow your mind to dwell on the emotions you felt. Identify them.

_____

_____

BBBBBBBBBBBBBBBBB   **BE WITH**   **BBBBBBBBBBBBBBBBBBB**

1. Be with what you felt. Using a metaphor or simile, describe what you felt.

    _____

    _____

2. Think carefully and recall the self-talk you used. Write what you were saying to yourself about the incident and your emotions.

    " _____

    _____ "

CCCCCCCCCCCCCCCCC   **CHANNEL**   **CCCCCCCCCCCCCCCCCCC**

1. Tell what you did with the emotion. Describe your actions.

    _____

    _____

2. Describe a better way to handle such an incident. Describe a more constructive way to express the emotion you felt.

    _____

    _____

*Permission granted to reproduce for classroom use. Taken from **Affective Self-Esteem** by Katherine Krefft, M.Ed., Ph.D. © 1993, Accelerated Development Inc., Publishers, 3808 W. Kilgore Avenue, Muncie, IN 47304-4896.*

Name: _____   Date: _____

Activity Sheet 3.2
SELF-TALK ANALYSIS FOR UPSETS

1. Describe an upsetting incident.

   _____

   _____

2. Describe your self-talk during the incident. Fill in as many of the following as apply. Don't forget quotation marks. If necessary, you may use the space on the back of this sheet.

   a. List self-talk that suggests you were frightened.

       " _____

       _____ "

   b. List self-talk that suggests you were angry or frustrated.

       " _____

       _____ "

   c. List self-talk that suggests you were sad or despondent.

       " _____

       _____ "

   d. List self-talk that suggests you were feeling guilty.

       " _____

       _____ "

   e. List self-talk that suggests you were feeling another emotion. Identify the emotion.

       " _____

       _____ "

3. Circle the self-talk above that most makes you feel disappointed in yourself. This particular self-talk may be followed by the self-talk, *"I shouldn't feel this way"* or *"I wish I didn't feel this way"* or *"It's terrible of me to feel this way."*

4. List some positive, constructive self-talk that may best help you to HANDLE IT. If you like, ask for help with this step.

   _____

   _____

*Permission granted to reproduce for classroom use. Taken from **Affective Self-Esteem** by Katherine Krefft, M.Ed., Ph.D.*
© 1993, Accelerated Development Inc., Publishers, 3808 W. Kilgore Avenue, Muncie, IN 47304-4896.

WORDS OF WIZARDRY

OBJECTIVES

Learners will demonstrate their comprehension of

1. the definition of self-talk, our "magic words," as revealed by discussing the correct use of the term, by writing the definition in their own words, and by giving examples from their own lives; and

2. the distinction between the feeling part of emotions and the thinking part of emotions and their components as displayed in activities on self-talk and garbage thinking.

MATERIALS

• Magic Wand

• Chalkboard or overhead projector

• A large garbage can

• Journals for learners

• Activity Sheet 4.1, "My Garbage Thinking"

CONTENT

1. **Review**

   Collect carryover assignment. Review the last lesson.

   • List the Magic A, B, C's.

   • What does "Allow the emotion" mean?

   • Explain what it means to "Be with" an emotion.

   • What are the two main ways to constructively channel emotions?

- What step of the A, B, C's is easiest for you?

- Which one is hardest?

- What verbal means of expression will you use?

- What nonverbal means will you use?

- What produces "butterflies in the stomach"?

- You and a friend are comforting a third friend who is upset. Your friend tells the distraught friend, *"It's all in your mind."* What do you say then?

- How have you used what you learned?

2. Self-talk: The Magic Words

The concept of **self-talk** is critical to constructive channeling of emotions and true self-possession. In these lessons the teacher is encouraged to use the term self-talk as often as possible with learners.

Some examples: *"And what self-talk were you using when you felt that way? Just before you hit your little brother, what was your self-talk? What was your self-talk when you began to get drunk last weekend? You just slammed your books down; what self-talk goes with that?"* When learners spontaneously refer to "my self-talk," the teacher will know a key learning objective has been achieved.

a. Definition and Rationale

Self-talk is thoughts. But the word "thoughts" is too passive a term to allow for active control. We know quite well that we think our own thoughts, but, generally, we like to believe thoughts happen TO us. We say, *"The thought just went through my head," "The thought came to me,"* and *"A troublesome thought keeps going through my mind."* Each statement **disowns** the thought.

Thus, the point of using the word, self-talk, is to stress to ourselves that we are responsible for our own thoughts. Self-talk that is emotionally charged does, at times, feel as if it is happening to us. By claiming our thoughts, even those generated by powerful emotion, we admit that we are in charge of both thinking and feeling.

b. What We Say In Our Heads

Explain to learners, *"Self-talk is what you say to yourself in your head about yourself and your world. When we say 'self-talk' instead of 'thoughts,' we remind ourselves that we are the ones responsible for what goes on in our own heads.*

"Self-talk is always YOUR self-talk and MY self-talk. Self-talk does not float around in the air until it 'goes through' someone's mind. Since it is MY self-talk, I have control. I put it there. I can change it. So can you. You can learn to change your self-talk and by changing it, change how you feel. In this way your self-talk is like your very own magic words."

Conduct class discussion. Have learners write their own definition of self-talk in their journals.

3. **The Thinking Part and the Feeling Part of Emotion**

Continue to describe the cognitive component of emotions. Explain simply, *"Each emotion has two parts, the **feeling part** and the **thinking part.**"* It may be helpful to put words in bold face on the board as you lead discussion.

a. **The Feeling Part**

Continue to explain, *"The feeling part of emotions is physiological. The feeling part is **IN THE BODY.**"*

- **In the Body**

  Continue, *"As we saw in the last lesson, the sensations we experience in an emotion are the result of complex physical changes. When we 'feel' an emotion, **hormones** are released that alter the biochemistry of the body. Then, **neurotransmitters** in the brain change, too."* If desired, the school science teacher may use this lesson as an opportunity to detail the biochemistry of emotion.

- **A Helpful Tip**

  Explain to learners that one way to get a grip on powerful emotions is to use self-talk like this, *"I'll be okay. It's only **the body's natural chemicals** in my brain and body. I will be okay."* Learners do not have to understand the body's biochemistry to use this technique.

- **Using Up the Hormones**

  Explain, *"Once emotion-connected hormones are released into the bloodstream, one **cannot will them away.** Hormones are real. Once an emotion happens, it must be expressed. Emotions do not evaporate because hormones do not do so.*

  *"Rather, the hormones **must be used up.** Expressing emotions in the ways already learned, for example, by **talking***

it out and in ***physical activity,*** *uses up the hormonal discharge. Even more, the constructive activity itself begins to alter the body's chemistry as when talking to a supportive friend settles us down."*

b. **The Thinking Part**

The cognitive part is ***mental.*** The thinking part is the self-talk ***IN THE MIND.*** We do not really know what we are feeling until we "talk to ourselves" about the experience. Research has proven that physiological arousal is greatly defined by the context and setting at the time of the arousal.

It helps to distinguish two types of self-talk, self-talk BEFORE the feeling and self-talk AFTER the feeling.

• **The BEFORE Self-talk**

Explain, *"The BEFORE self-talk often flashes through the mind so rapidly that we are **not consciously aware** of it. Perhaps 70% of constructive self-control of emotions is figuring out just what that **secret, 'magic' self-talk** is. Once we do that, the other 30%—how to appropriately express the emotion—is relatively easy.*

*"Emotions seem spontaneous to us ('I can't help how I feel') because ordinarily we are not aware of the self-talk that comes **before** the emotion. For example, two students walk down the hall between classes. A third hustles along and steps on the toes of first one, then the other.*

"The first student lets out a stream of obscenity and then screams, 'Who do you think you are?' The second one yells, 'Owww' and nothing more. Why the difference?"

Pass the wand to elicit learners' input. Then, go on to explain that the difference is the unconscious self-talk of the two wounded students. The first has self-talk along the lines of, *"Anyone who moves into my personal space does so on purpose just to attack or offend me. No one has the right to do that!"* Thus the shout, *"Who do you think you are?"*

The question really means, *"You are not someone who has a right to enter my personal space. Get off my toe."* The anger results from a ***belief*** that one's "rights" have been maliciously abrogated. Explain to learners that this is an example of ***garbage thinking.***

The second wounded student, on the other hand, does not possess the same inner self-talk. This student has self-talk such as, *"Accidents happen. In a crowded hallway toes sometimes get stepped on. It's no one's fault; it's no big deal." "Owww" means "It hurts"* and nothing more.

The second student's self-talk accurately reflects reality. Garbage thinking does not. Garbage self-talk is thinking replete with highly personalized exaggerations and errors in reasoning.

- **The AFTER Self-talk**

The self-talk that comes AFTER is critical to either ending or continuing the emotional experience. The student who believes, *"Accidents happen, no big deal,"* will quickly get over the incident. No additional emotions generate.

But Mr. Mad At The World cannot let it go. The *"How dare you!"* **garbage self-talk** repeats and renews the experience. This is what is called **nursing a hurt.** To each fresh wave of anger he responds with another variation of *"I've been attacked, my rights violated."*

This building of anger is called **working up a good mad.** We TALK ourselves into a good mad. We talk ourselves into being scared to death. We talk ourselves into being *"so guilty I can't stand it."* We talk ourselves into depression by dwelling on sadness, guilt, and rage. We talk ourselves into alcohol abuse and drug use. We may talk ourselves all the way to suicide if we just keep talking long enough.

BUT, by the same token, we may talk ourselves OUT of suicide and other inappropriate expressions of emotion. A strong emotion keeps the tape recorder of garbage self-talk playing over and over. To stop the tape, we must first relieve these emotions; we must follow the A, B, C's.

4. **Summary**

To summarize: The BEFORE self-talk is the **secret** "magic" self-talk, our own magic words to feeling or not feeling the emotion. The AFTER self-talk determines whether we will stop the emotion or continue it. We have no magic to instantly zap away those troublesome hormones. But even if we cannot instantly change the feeling part, we CAN change the thinking part.

No matter how strong the emotion, we always have the magic power to determine our own self-talk. That takes hard work and practice. Being able to identify and change self-talk is a **learned** process. That learning is the purpose of AFFECTIVE SELF-ESTEEM.

Even though we cannot instantly zap hormones, we may learn to use natural approaches such as slow breathing and meditation to alter body chemistry. Evidence is growing that we use drugs like alcohol to "zap" away uncomfortable physiological feelings that accompany challenging emotions (Dr. Robert J. Pandina, Rutgers University, 1990; see Introduction). Drugs succeed in zapping the hormones, but zap our Selves in the process.

ACTIVITIES

Choose one or a combination. Assign one for carryover.

1. **Journaling—Finding My Self-talk**

   Direct learners, *"Go back over the story you wrote in your journal for the last lesson. Find your self-talk and underline it. If it's not there in so many words, then write it out on the next page."* Share results in class.

2. **"My Garbage Thinking"**
   (Activity 4.1)

   Complete the activity sheet. Results may be shared in class. As an added touch, have learners tear off the bottom of the sheet and staple it in their journals. Then have them crumple the upper "garbage" portion and throw it in the garbage can. As each learner does so, he/she may say out loud the one item of garbage self-talk above all others that he/she wants to be rid of.

3. **Find The Magic Words**

   Using the story titles in Lesson 3, Activity 1, have learners verbally make up a short tale. Other learners "guess" what unspoken self-talk generated the emotion.

   This is similar to Activity 1, but this time the story teller does not have to identify the self-talk. *"Just tell the story; don't worry about the self-talk."* The other learners listen. When the story teller is finished, they "find the magic words," that is, they say what they think could be the self-talk. "Find The Magic Words" should generate as much laughter as insight.

BULLETIN BOARD MATERIAL

1. Give yourself a good talking to.

2. Find the Magic Words!

3. Garbage thinking is junky self-talk.

Name: _____   Date: _____

Activity Sheet 4.1.
MY GARBAGE THINKING

List your self-talk in each area. Then, draw a garbage can around the top three lists of self-talk!

Things I say to myself
That are guaranteed to make me angry:

" _____
_____
_____
_____ "

Things I say to myself
That are guaranteed to make me sad:

" _____
_____
_____
_____ "

Things I say to myself
That are guaranteed to make me scared:

" _____
_____
_____
_____ "

Things I say to myself
That are guaranteed to make me happy:

" _____
_____
_____
_____ "

Permission granted to reproduce for classroom use. Taken from **Affective Self-Esteem** *by Katherine Krefft, M.Ed., Ph.D.*
© *1993, Accelerated Development Inc., Publishers, 3808 W. Kilgore Avenue, Muncie, IN 47304-4896.*

UNIT II:
ANGER

THE DRAGON

OBJECTIVES

Learners will demonstrate their comprehension of

1. how to apply the A, B, C's of constructive emotional expression to anger as shown by giving examples from society and from their own lives;

2. the two paths of anger as revealed by class discussion and exercises that differentiate the two paths; and

3. verbal and physical expressions of anger in society and in their lives as demonstrated by sharing examples of those expressions.

MATERIALS

- Magic Wand

- Chalkboard or overhead projector

- Journals for learners

- Activity Sheets 5.1, "List of Anger Words" and 5.2, "The A Word"

CONTENT

1. **Review**

   Collect carryover assignment. Review the last lesson.

   - What is self-talk?

   - Why do we say "self-talk" instead of "thoughts"?

   - Did your self-talk talk you into trouble this week?

   - Describe and explain the two parts of emotion.

- Describe some useful self-talk that may help us get a grip on powerful emotions.

- Explain why a felt emotion must be expressed.

- Why don't emotions just evaporate?

- What is **Before Self-talk?** Why is it "magic"?

- What would you say if someone said, *"I can't help the way I feel?"*

- What is **After Self-talk?**

- How does **After Self-talk** continue an emotion?

- How do people talk themselves into suicide? Into drug abuse? Into getting drunk?

- How have you used what you have learned?

- Close your eyes. What is on the bulletin board?

2. Anger: The Powerhouse Emotion

Begin with, *"Now let's look at one of our most challenging emotions, anger. Learning to constructively manage and channel anger transforms misery to magic. All magicians have 'secrets,' and I'm going to tell you one: Anger is the powerhouse Nature gave us. The positive use of anger is* **determination.**

"We all need to be powerful sometimes. Inside all of us is the sleeping dragon of anger, and that dragon's name is Determination. Your Magic Dragon is there to help you get what you want and need out of life."

Continue to explore the positive and negative implications of anger. *"If emotions in general are like water, can you think of something in nature that might be said to be like anger?"* Pass the wand from learner to learner for answers. Accept any appropriate answer. In particular, from time immemorial in myths and folktales *fire* has been used as an image for anger.

Elicit from learners the **positive** and **negative** sides of fire. Fire under control may warm a home and cook food. Out of control it may burn down a house or forest. *"So, is fire good or bad?"* Lead learners to see that, obviously, it is neither. It depends on how it is used.

Continue the analogy, *"What about anger? Is it good or bad?"* Learners will see from the analogy that anger is neither good nor bad. It depends on how it is used.

3. **The Two Paths of Anger**

As you continue to lead the discussion, place the following diagram on the board.

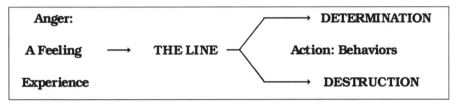

Explain that just as emotion has a **thinking part** and a **feeling part** and **Before** and **After** self-talk, we may also contrast **experiencing** the emotion with **acting on it.** At some point in the total encounter with the emotion, we cross over **THE LINE** between feeling and acting.

As you elicit learners' input, circle the words, "THE LINE," on the board. Continue, *"There is all the difference in the world between feeling angry and acting on that anger. It all depends on how you cross THE LINE. Just feeling angry, even ragefully angry, is one thing. But **destructively** acting out anger is not acceptable. Feeling angry is okay. Acting with hostility is not."*

Lead learners in a discussion of the two ways to cross the line from feeling angry to action. The first is the **constructive** path of **determination.** The second is the **destructive** path of **hostility.** Hostility is animosity actively expressed. Hostility is destructive because **hostility creates more hostility** in a cycle that, quite literally, may be never ending.

But anger does not have to end in empty, futile acts that only succeed in creating more anger. Anger must have some long-term survival value or it would not be part of our make-up. The value of anger is that, rightly used and directed, anger creates determination.

Determination is **resolute** action of **tenacious** steadfastness. Determination is not solely an attitude. It is **action.** It is positive action taken up with conviction and pursued come what may. Anger directed to create positive, just, and equitable outcomes is sometimes called **righteous anger.** The organization Mothers Against Drunk Driving with its poignant acronym, M.A.D.D., is a perfect example of the constructive force of such anger.

4. **The A, B, C's and Anger**

Now apply the key concepts learned in the first four lessons to anger exclusively. *"Let's consider some times we got angry in light of what we now know about emotions."*

Using examples supplied by learners, relate the A, B, C's of constructive emotional expression to anger. Continue, *"What are some verbal ways we express anger?"*

a. **Verbal Hostility**

Allow learners to discuss the usual, familiar modes of verbal anger expression including cursing, swearing, and name-calling. These are common forms of ***verbal hostility.***

Lead learners in understanding that all hostility builds walls. Verbal hostility does express the emotion, but it destroys communication, blocks logical thinking, and stimulates more angry words. Hostility is not okay.

b. **Positive Verbal Expression**

Ask learners, *"What might be a more positive verbal means to express anger?"* Lead learners to see that direct expression is best. However, most of us as children did not learn the language of positive, direct expression of anger. Constructive verbal expression of emotion is ***learned*** just as verbal hostility is a learned behavior.

Positive verbal expression of anger uses ***I language.*** I language is a statement that uses the word "I." It is the opposite of blaming which uses the word "you." A model statement of positive verbal anger expression is, *"I am feeling very angry with you."*

As the wand moves around the classroom, engage learners in a role play of past encounters with anger. Direct learners to use I language to express the anger as two or three learners role play the incident. If a learner "slips" and uses "you," be quick to point out how hard it is to be angry and not blame someone else.

Direct expression is not always possible, e.g., when a policeman stops you. However, talking it out with a friend is *usually* a possible and constructive expression of anger.

5. **Constructive versus Destructive Physical Expressions**

Continue, *"What about physical expressions of anger?"* These are legion. Allow learners to recite the catalog from pinching and biting all the way to murder. *"Okay, we have to admit that's how we human beings express our anger. What happens when we allow ourselves to indulge in such overt hostility?"*

Accept all appropriate responses such as society is chaotic and belligerent, innocent people are hurt, no one is safe, and people go to jail. A society's system of law is in good part a collective attempt to curtail and regulate destructive physical expressions of anger. In a free society angry speech is acceptable. Angry acts, by and large, are not.

a. **Physical Expressions**

Direct the discussion onto constructive physical expressions of anger. *"Let's think of **positive** ways to express anger. We've said that anger is our Magic Dragon. It can be like a powerful furnace, our own powerhouse for making things happen. First, let's look at society as a whole. What positive expressions of anger do you see?"*

b. **Athletics**

Continue, *"How is anger useful in athletics?"* Elicit from learners how getting psyched up for a game brings more powerful play. Discuss sports as a whole as society's major mass outlet for anger. This does not mean that all athletes as individuals are angry people. However, hockey and soccer games often demonstrate the thin line between appropriate anger release and overt hostility.

Finally, ask, *"Do you use sports to express your anger? If not, why not? What sport could you use?"* Pass the wand as learners respond. Clarify that aggression and hostility are anger directed outward, anger acted upon. Sports and other competitions are socially approved methods of such expression. Aggressive play on the ball field is okay—up to a point. The referee, the coach, the rules of the game decide just what that point is.

ACTIVITIES

Choose one or a combination. Assign one for carryover.

1. **The Person Who Went Berserk**

Write title on the chalkboard. Instruct learners, *"Together we're going to tell a story about a person who went berserk. I'll begin. Each of you will add a line. Everyone will have two or three turns (depending on class size). Let's make it the angriest, silliest tale we can invent. Ready? Here we go. Once there was a very, **very** quiet person."*

After the group has had some good laughs, explain, *"Laughing at our anger is the very BEST way to transform it into a powerhouse for good."*

2. **Journaling**

If learners have difficulty with spontaneous invention, have them first write the story from Activity 1 in their journals. Then, orally combine elements from the written stories.

3. **Social Studies Research**

Integrate the lesson with history, the record of how nations have expressed angry hostility. Discuss wars of aggression versus wars of defense to show how anger works on a societal level. For additional input see Lesson Twenty-One.

4. **Aggressive versus Determined Leaders**

Use biographies of famous leaders to illustrate how nations and persons express anger, e.g., compare and contrast Hitler and Churchill. How were they alike? (Both were famous for great rages.) How were they different?

Churchill was no less of an angry man, but he used his anger to save Britain and Europe, not for blatant aggression. His *"We will fight on the beaches . . . we will never surrender!"* speech is a supreme example of anger turned into a powerhouse of determined, positive action. Winston Churchill's Magic Dragon saved Britain.

5. **"List of Anger Words," Activity One**
   (Activity Sheet 5.1)

Assign learners to write a story, "One Day I Was a Little Mad," using the List of Anger Words. In this first lesson on anger instruct that they use only words from the *first* column. In lessons to come they will use the other columns.

Instruct learners, *"Write a story about a time you were a LITTLE angry. As you relate the story, use at least ten words from the FIRST column."* State your requirements for English usage: correct grammar, spelling, organization, and so on. Stories may be shared in class.

If appropriate for your setting, the Language Arts teacher may supervise the writing tasks in these lessons.

6. **"The 'A' Word"**
   (Activity Sheet 5.2)

Instruct learners to complete the sheet. Discuss results as a class or in small groups. The exercise may be expanded by making posters that detail all the statements in each area, e.g., "Our Class' Best Whining," "Our Class' Best Blaming," and "Our Class' Best Threats."

BULLETIN BOARD MATERIAL

1. When you get mad, get motivated.

2. Anger is a Magic Dragon named Determination.

3. Anger is okay. Hostility is not.

Name: _____   Date: _____

Activity Sheet 5.1.
LIST OF ANGER WORDS

MILD ANGER	MODERATE ANGER	INTENSE ANGER
aggravated	mad	inflamed
put out	irate	fuming
impatient	frustrated	infuriated
testy	petulant	surly
condescending	contemptuous	disdainful
contentious	belligerent	bellicose
cross	fractious	cantankerous
grouchy	peevish	crabby
annoyed	indignant	incensed
ticked off	irritated	bitter
offended	affronted	insulted
pushy	aggressive	pugnacious
piqued	inflamed	seething
irked	vexed	enraged
miffed	rankled	rant and rave
pestered	exasperated	deranged
smoldering	riled up	berserk
insolent	defiant	rebellious
pouting	sulking	grumbling
chafing	brooding	resentful
oversensitive	irritable	irascible
touchy	cranky	quarrelsome
crusty	crotchety	churlish
worked up	wrought up	furious
wrathful	hostile	warring
harsh	truculent	combative
biting	scathing	vitriolic
brutal	vicious	ferocious
abrupt	curt	brusque
mean	cruel	ruthless
sarcastic	mocking	scornful
sardonic	cynical	satirical
tart	acrimonious	caustic
acrid	astringent	virulent
smirk	sneer	scoff
deride	cutting	taunt
sharp	brutish	acerbic
beastly	vehement	vicious
fierce	violent	savage

Permission granted to reproduce for classroom use. Taken from **Affective Self-Esteem** *by Katherine Krefft, M.Ed., Ph.D.* © *1993, Accelerated Development Inc., Publishers, 3808 W. Kilgore Avenue, Muncie, IN 47304-4896.*

Name: _____   Date: _____

Activity Sheet 5.2
THE "A" WORD

Are people ANGRY at you more often than you like? If so, examining how you talk to others may help. Circle the items that are similar to the talk you use. Write your own statements, too.

1. **DEMANDING AND WHINING**

   "I told you to do it *now!*"
   "Aw, why don't you buy me new jeans."
   "You better not say another word."
   "She always gets more cookies than I do."

   My favorite demanding and whining statement(s):

   _____

   _____

   _____

   _____

   _____

   _____

2. **JUDGING AND BLAMING**

   "You should have known better."
   "You never know when to quit."
   "Now you've done it! You ought to be ashamed."
   "Well, what else should I have expected from you?"
   "It's all your fault!"

   My favorite judging and blaming statement(s):

   _____

   _____

   _____

   _____

   _____

   _____

*Permission granted to reproduce for classroom use. Taken from **Affective Self-Esteem** by Katherine Krefft, M.Ed., Ph.D. © 1993, Accelerated Development Inc., Publishers, 3808 W. Kilgore Avenue, Muncie, IN 47304-4896.*

Name: _____   Date: _____

Activity Sheet 5.2 (Continued)

3. **NAME CALLING**

   "You dingbat nerd."
   "You clumsy fool."
   "You stupid idiot."

   My favorite name calling statement(s):

   _____

   _____

   _____

   _____

   _____

   _____

   _____

   _____

   _____

4. **THREATENING**

   "If you do that again, I'll beat the #@*! out of you."

   "Why don't you watch where you're going?"

   "How'd you like it if I did that to you?"

   "You're going to get it!"

   My favorite threatening statement(s):

   _____

   _____

   _____

   _____

   _____

   _____

   _____

   _____

Permission granted to reproduce for classroom use. Taken from **Affective Self-Esteem** *by Katherine Krefft, M.Ed., Ph.D.* © 1993, Accelerated Development Inc., Publishers, 3808 W. Kilgore Avenue, Muncie, IN 47304-4896.

HOW THE DRAGON FEELS AND THINKS

OBJECTIVES

Learners will demonstrate their comprehension of

1. angry self-talk and how it induces and maintains anger as demonstrated by class discussion and written exercises,

2. the thinking versus the feeling part of anger as evidenced by initiating the writing of an Anger Management Plan in their journals, and

3. the difference between Before and After angry self-talk as manifested by their correct use of self-talk in examples shared in class and written in the activities.

MATERIALS

- Magic Wand

- Chalkboard or overhead projector

- Pictures of great leaders or their names

- Pictures of anger expression

- Journals for learners

- Activity Sheets 5.1, "List of Anger Words," and 6.1, "Ex-hostage Used Anger To Survive"

CONTENT

1. **Review**

    a. Review the major concepts taught to date.

    - Facts versus feelings
    - Misunderstandings, myths

NOTES

- Emotions are like water
- The head versus the heart
- Comfortable emotions
- Uncomfortable emotions
- The A, B, C's
- Step C: verbal, nonverbal
- Thinking part of emotion
- Feeling part of emotion
- Self-talk
- Before/after self-talk

b. Collect carryover assignment. Review the last lesson.

- Why do we call anger the Magic Dragon?

- How is anger like fire?

- Describe the Two Paths of Anger. What is THE LINE?

- Refer to the diagram. What is anger like on the left side of THE LINE? On the right side of THE LINE?

- Why is hostility a poor way to express anger?

- How may anger be constructively used?

- Relate the A, B, C's to anger expression.

- Describe constructive and destructive ways to verbally express anger. To nonverbally express anger.

- What is "I language"? When should we use it?

- Describe an incident when you channeled anger into determination to help you get what you wanted.

2. **How Anger Feels in the Body**

a. **Temper Tantrums**

Explain to learners that anger is challenging because knowing how to constructively manage it is an ability that is LEARNED. Ask, *"How does a two-year-old show anger?"* Pass the wand around as learners respond. Elicit a full description of the average temper tantrum.

Continue, *"How does a young child come to stop throwing tantrums? Have you thrown a temper tantrum lately? How do tantrums thrown by older folks differ from those thrown by pre-schoolers? How are they the same?"*

The discussion will show that when we are intensely angry, the natural impulse is to **move our limbs.** The two-year-old's temper tantrum is a riot of flying arms and legs. Physical movement helps discharge the tension.

b. Fighting and Other "Adult" Temper Tantrums

Explain to learners that growing up is a steady process of moving from inappropriate expressions like tantrums to more acceptable expressions. However, that impulse to move the limbs is difficult to overcome. Society is full of double messages about what is and what is not acceptable adult anger expression. While we pay lip service to the idea that fighting is unacceptable, movies and TV are replete with violent heros that model fighting as manly and tough. Tantrums by any other name are still tantrums.

The result is that youngsters are confused and ambivalent about how to demonstrate that they are strong and "tough." Pass the wand around as you probe this issue with questions similar to these:

- How do you feel when you get into a fight?

- How do you feel *in your body* while you are fighting?

- And after the fight is over?

- Whether you win or lose, how do you feel *in your mind?* How do you feel about yourself?

- What effect does drinking have on fighting?

- What does getting stoned do to anger?

- Do you like the idea that other people see you as the kind of person who starts or gets into fights?

- Do YOU want to be around a person like that?

Continue to review the positive (self-defense) and negative implications of violent anger expression.

3. Visualization of an Angry Episode

Continue with a visualization exercise. *"Close your eyes and think about a time you were really, really angry. See the person, the situation. See it as clearly as if it were a movie. See yourself and what you said and did. (Pause.) Now turn off the movie and focus instead on your body. Look for the tension and uncomfortable physical sensations. (Pause.) Okay, now open your eyes. What was your body doing while your mind was mad?"*

If learners find it difficult to respond, probe with, *"Remember the feeling part of emotion is the physiological part. How did the* anger FEEL in your body? What were all those little hormones and chemicals doing to your body?"

a. Humor

If learners are resistant or resort to joking about how anger feels, share that these responses are defenses. *"Yes, it's scary to talk about how anger feels. It's a lot easier to make jokes about it. In fact, humor is an excellent way to dissolve anger, to lighten up, and not take our anger so seriously."*

Explain that humor is one way to use up the hormonal discharges connected with anger—as long as we truly dissolve the anger and do not just cover it up. After a hearty laugh, ask, *"Is the anger really gone?"* If not, talk about it directly by saying, *"I'm angry that—"* and name the anger, specifically, clearly.

b. Other Expressions

Continue with, *"How else, besides humor, may we use up the physical discharge anger creates?"* Some acceptable expressions are to run around the block, punch a pillow, clean out a closet, play a vigorous sport, talk it out, paint an angry picture, and/or play music. Ask, *"What music do you listen to that is angry music?"* Elicit comments on lyrics and rhythms of popular songs that demonstrate constructive and nonconstructive expressions of anger.

4. The Dragon's Mind

As for all emotions, the cognitive part of anger is mental: the self-talk that precedes and follows the physiological anger.

Explain that since we talk ourselves into anger, we may talk ourselves out. To do so we must **be honest** about the context and setting that instigate the anger. Doing so is the challenge: being angry is easier than being honest.

a. Angry Self-talk

Both the BEFORE Self-talk and the AFTER Self-talk must be identified to get to the root of the anger. Remind learners that the Before Self-talk of the anger is often below the level of conscious awareness.

Continue, *"Now think again of that time you got really, really angry. What was your **self-talk JUST BEFORE** you got angry? Think, think hard. It's **your** mind so you **can** dig it out. Why did you get so angry?"*

b. **Examples**

Proceed to discuss examples of anger-generating self-talk. As the next lesson will show, a common type of self-talk that precedes anger is of the "It's Not Fair" variety. To say to oneself "I'm not being treated fairly" is to guarantee a good mad. Remind learners that the Before Self-talk is the *secret "magic" self-talk,* the magic words to feeling or not feeling the anger.

The **AFTER self-talk** determines whether we will stop the anger. The After Self-talk clearly demonstrates that each individual is in charge. Each of us is in full control. To continue to be angry or to release anger are our choices.

5. **I Am the Victim of my Anger**

Lead learners in a discussion of the many ways that negative expressions of anger generate negative results. Hostility produces *negative consequences.*

a. **Painful Social Consequences**

Hostility *disrupts relationships* and leads to the failure of the family as our primary support system. It *destroys compassion* and love. It damages the family, society's most fundamental unit. Extreme consequences range from social ostracism to *imprisonment* or worse.

b. **My Hostility Destroys ME**

Besides "getting into trouble" and other unpleasant social consequences, lead learners to see that I MYSELF always suffer the worst from negative expressions of anger.

This occurs in at least three ways:

(1) Intense hostility creates uncomfortable physiological sensations *in MY body.* MY hostility may physically harm someone else, but it also always harms ME. Those who make revenge a way of life usually end by destroying themselves—literally.

Recent medical research reveals that Type 2 personalities (formerly called Type A) have more coronary heart disease. Such individuals see an external person or object as a continuing anger-provoking source. Long-term anger, irritation, and perceived helplessness result. Carefully done studies show that Type 2's have more heart attacks and strokes.[2] This presents an intriguing metaphor: In attacking others, we attack our own hearts.

---

[2] Grossarth-Maticek, R., & Eysenck, H.J. (1992, February). "Psychological factors in the prognosis, prophylaxis, and treatment of cancer and coronary heart disease." *Directions in Clinical Psychology, Volume 2, Lesson 2* (pp. 2-1 to 2-17). New York: The Hatherleigh Co., Ltd. The article lists twenty references, most dated post 1987, that document the research. For further information, write The American Psychological Association, 750 First St., N.E., Washington, D.C. 20002.

(2) Hostility lowers **MY self-esteem.** Most people do not want to see themselves as angry. Nor do they want others to see them as "an angry, hateful person." Again, angry acts may hurt someone else, but MY self-hatred for those acts always hurts ME.

(3) Hostility **boomerangs.** Aggressive acts create more aggressive acts. Sooner or later, the hostility comes back to its source. *"What goes around, comes around."* Classic fairy tales and myths are replete with examples of evil witches and wizards who attempt to destroy others but in the end a boomerang of self-destruction occurs.

ACTIVITIES

Choose one or a combination. Assign one for carryover.

1. **Journaling—The Hostage**

   Assign learners to read the story of Robert Polhill (Activity Sheet 6.1). Instruct learners, *"Imagine that **you** are a hostage. You keep a journal. Write four entries in which you express the self-talk you use to survive mentally, emotionally, and physically. How does a hostage express the thinking part of anger? The physical part of anger?"*

   Have learners trade journals and comment on what they feel is constructive versus destructive self-talk. The exercise may be correlated with Anne Frank's story, *The Diary of a Young Girl* (B. M. Mooyaart-Doubleday, translator. New York: Pocket Books, 1952), a beautiful record of positive self-talk expressed in the most trying of circumstances.

2. **The Self-talk of X**

   Show learners pictures of great world leaders of today and yesterday who suffered some unfairness in life. Some examples are Lincoln, Ghandi, King, Harriet Tubman, Helen Keller, Vaclav Havel, Lech Walesa, Nelson and Winny Mandela. Well-known athletes like Magic Johnson and other celebrities may be included. Have each learner choose one and write two kinds of self-talk for that person.

   For the first direct learners, *"First, write the kind of self-talk you think this person used when he/she was feeling low. Write what you think they might have said to make themselves even more miserable."*

   Second, instruct learners, *"Then, on another sheet write the self-talk you think they used to pick themselves up and get themselves out of their anger. When things were darkest, what positive things did they say to themselves?"*

As a variant, the teacher may assign a picture to groups of two or three learners who then work together to complete the assignment.

3. My Personal Anger Management Plan, Part I

Instruct learners, *"We're going to begin to work on our own, personalized Anger Management Plans. Choose a page in your journal and save at least three pages behind it. On the first page write 'My Own Anger Management Plan.' "* Put the words on the chalkboard. Learners write the words at the top of the first sheet. Other sheets will be for future use.

"We'll begin by writing some helpful self-talk and so we'll call it, Help Talk." Instruct learners to write Help Talk as a subhead on the first sheet. Remind learners of the self-talk that helps remind us that anger is physical, such as, *"I'll be okay. It's only the chemicals in my brain and body. I will be okay."*

Continue, *"Now write your own Help Talk to remind yourself that anger is a physical thing. Give a **name** to the physical side of your anger, like 'Mr. Hormone' or something like that. Think about it, and I'm sure you can come up with some really good names for the physical side of your anger."*

Learners write their own Help Talk in which they address the physical side of anger by the invented names. Remind learners that all self-talk begins and ends with quotation marks to show it is our own inner dialogue or monologue, what we actually *say* to ourselves.

4. "List of Anger Words," Activity Two (Activity Sheet 5.1)

Assign learners to write a story, "When I Was Mad," using the List of Anger Words from the last lesson. In this second lesson on anger instruct them to use the words from the *second* column. Instruct learners, *"Relate a story about a time you were MODERATELY angry, more than a little angry but not furious. As you tell the story, use at least ten words from the second column of your List of Anger Words."* As before, state your requirements for good English or coordinate with the Language Arts teacher.

As a variant, instruct, *"In your story use as many words from the second column, and only the second column, as you can. We'll have a contest and see who uses the most words in good sentences that make sense."* The teacher, learners, or participants from another class may judge the contest.

Learners who desire may illustrate the stories.

5. **I Imagine**

Collect pictures of angry, aggressive acts and hostile people. Have learners write paragraphs to describe the nature of the anger. The paragraphs begin, *"I imagine this person is [angry] because . . . ."* In describing the anger learners use the List of Anger Words to fill in the brackets. For example, *"I imagine this person is peeved because,"* and *"I imagine this person is irritated because,"* and so on.

BULLETIN BOARD MATERIAL

1.
What's it all about?
When in doubt,
Talk it out!

2.
The Rule About Anger:
No matter how angry I ever get,
It's not okay to hit someone.

Name: _____   Date: _____

Activity Sheet 6.1
EX-HOSTAGE USED ANGER TO SURVIVE

Iran Calls for Release of Another

Damascus, Syria (AP)—A gaunt, pale Robert Polhill was freed Sunday by pro-Iranian Shiite Moslem militants in Beirut after 1,182 days as a hostage, and he said his anger kept him alive.

He was the first American hostage to be released in nearly 3^1/$_2$ years.

In Iran, a newspaper close to Iranian President Hashemi Rafsanjani said Monday that the Lebanese kidnappers should release another American hostage immediately without conditions.

Polhill, 55, of New York, was freed near the seaside Summerland Hotel in Moslem west Beirut at 5:15 p.m. (11:15 a.m. EDT) and driven immediately to Damascus where he was turned over to U.S. Ambassador Edward Djerejian.

"I want to tell you I'm a very happy man tonight," Polhill told a news conference in Damascus, looking dazed but elated...."

Polhill said he played cards with other hostages during his captivity and tried to keep his mind off the possibility of freedom.

"I strived to continue to be angry, knowing at all times that if I began to lose that anger I would just sort of become a vegetable and I didn't want that to happen," he said in the interview...."

Polhill, a professor of business studies and accounting at Beirut University College, joked to reporters: "Thirty-nine months is a long time to have to stand here."

Standing beside Polhill, Djerejian said: "We will keep communication lines open to all parties that have influence with the hostage takers. We are going to continue doing everything we can, we are going to continue talking, to continue trying."

Also speaking at the news conference, Syria's foreign minister, Farouk al-Sharaa, said he hoped Polhill's release "will be just the beginning of the release of the rest of the hostages."

Excerpted from *The Post-Standard*, Monday, April 23, 1990, pages A-1 and A-6, Syracuse, NY.

*Permission granted to reproduce for classroom use. Taken from **Affective Self-Esteem** by Katherine Krefft, M.Ed., Ph.D. © 1993, Accelerated Development Inc., Publishers, 3808 W. Kilgore Avenue, Muncie, IN 47304-4896.*

THE THREE GREMLINS OF ANGER

OBJECTIVES

Learners will demonstrate their comprehension of

1. the meaning of threat, fact, belief, egotism, and ego as illustrated by class discussion and by definitions written in their journals;

2. the definitions of and the differences and similarities among the Three Gremlins of Anger as demonstrated by oral discussions and written exercises; and

3. their own personal Anger Management Plan as revealed by adding to the plan a page, My Special Gremlin.

MATERIALS

- Magic Wand

- Chalkboard or overhead projector

- Dictionaries

- Journals for learners

- Activity Sheets 5.1, "List of Anger Words," and 7.1, "Action Plan for Challenges"

CONTENT

1. **Review**

   Collect carryover assignment. Review the last lesson.

   - In what ways is anger like a Magic Dragon?

   - How does anger help us get what we need or want?

- List some negative consequences of inappropriate expressions of anger.

- How does your anger hurt *you?*

- What natural phenomenon is anger like and why?

- List some verbal and non-verbal ways we express anger.

- What are the two parts of anger?

- List some constructive ways to use up the physical discharge, the feeling part of anger.

- Name the two kinds of self-talk that make up the thinking part of anger. Describe them.

- How have you used what you have learned?

- Close your eyes. What is on the bulletin board?

2. **Threats in General**

   a. **Definition**

      According to the dictionary, a threat is

      (1) an expression of intention to punish or hurt or harm;

      (2) an indication of something undesirable;

      (3) a person or thing regarded as liable to bring danger or catastrophe (*Oxford American Dictionary*, New York: Oxford University Press, 1980, page 714).

      Thus, a threat may be something "regarded as liable" to bring harm as well as that which is actually harmful. The distinction is important because we frequently do get angry about things that cannot really hurt us. A BELIEF that something is harmful is sufficient to generate anger.

   b. **Facts vs. Beliefs**

      Explain the difference between a **fact** and a **belief.** *"What is a fact? What is a belief?"* If necessary, direct, *"Well, let's get out the dictionary and see what it says about the difference."*

      Sum up the discussion. *"So, a belief is essentially an opinion. When it comes to anger, our **beliefs** about what is and is not threatening are all important. Let's begin by looking at three causes of anger that affect most people. We call them the Three Gremlins of Anger."*

3. **Three Causes of Anger**

   a. **The First Anger Gremlin: Threats to Self**

      The first cause of anger, the first gremlin, is the Gremlin of Threats to Self. By this we mean the threat of physical danger, the threat, real or imagined, of actual **physical harm.**

The presence of harm is both a real danger and a threat for until the danger is actually deadly, it remains a threat to physical life. So, by threat to self we mean all real and present **dangers** and those **things potentially dangerous** in the same way.

Put on the chalkboard, Gremlin 1: Threats to Self (Real Dangers). Ask, *"What are some threats to self? Let's make a list of threats to self."* Pass the wand as learners share ideas by writing them on the board. Then, go over the list, item by item, and elicit from learners the types of emotion appropriate for each. Note the frequency of fear and anger as normal responses to tangible threats.

Gremlin 1: Threats to Self (Real Dangers)

For example, automobile accident may be near the top of the list. Ask, *"And what emotions would you feel if you were in an automobile accident? What emotion would you feel just before the crash? What emotion would you feel just after the crash—supposing you were alive and conscious? What emotion would you feel three days after the accident? If you had been seriously injured, what emotion would you feel three months after the accident? At what point would you be scared? At what point would you be angry? What about other emotions? Grief? Guilt?"*

In the above discussion be sensitive to learners who actually have endured a real threat. Guide the discussion so that learners who have not personally experienced the extremes of severe physical danger may understand their relative safety. On the other hand, if you are teaching these lessons in an environment such as an inner city, accept learners' examples that describe the sad but real plight of frequent threats to self.

Learners may leap ahead into Threats to Ego and Fairness. Use this natural progression to move on.

b. **The Second Anger Gremlin: Threats to Ego**

In this day and age most people do not experience extreme or unusual threats to their physical safety on a daily basis. Certainly, we take our lives into our hands every time we drive or cross a street. However, for the most part we rely on the safety of our vehicles and our own expertise to give us reasonable protection.

Contrast this lack of physical danger with the frequency of threats to ego. The Ego Gremlin is everywhere. This gremlin lurks in the corridors of every business, school, and home. For some people almost daily threats to ego generate great anger on a daily basis.

Gremlin 2: Threats to Ego

NOTES

(1) Ego

Explain to learners, *"By the word, ego, we mean more than is usually meant when someone says, 'You're egotistical,' or 'You're an egotist.' What do we mean by these words?"* If necessary, pass the wand to a learner to again consult the dictionary. *"And how does egoism differ in meaning from ego?"* The words are found close together in the dictionary.

In these lessons we give the word, ego, an extended and enriched definition. Thus, continue, *"So, by ego we mean our sense of **self-esteem** and **self-worth.** As we are going to use it, ego means our **sense of who we are.***

*Ego is a function in our minds that tells us who we are and who we are not. It is a **mental self,** a sense of where personal self stops and connection with others, the collective self, begins. By ego, then, we mean our **individuality,** our individual sense of self."*

(2) Assaults to Ego

Explain to learners that just as the physical self may be attacked and subjected to harm, the non-physical, mental self, the ego, may also be threatened. Assaults, real and imagined, to self-esteem, independence, and individuality constitute the second gremlin, the Gremlin of Threats to Ego. List, Gremlin 2: Threats to Ego, on the chalkboard. As above, elicit from learners an appropriate list.

The list should compile examples of **humiliation, shaming,** and **put-downs** in general. Do not forget to include belittling **name calling,** a favorite put-down among teens. Use lists generated in the last lesson or do that activity at this point. Sum up by asking what emotion is stimulated by each item on the board. Anger will lead the list, followed closely by what is usually called hurt.

Hurt is a highly personal grief tinged with anxiety. The grief is the sadness of **mourning** lost self-esteem and the pain of losing face with others. The anxiety is often a trace of fear that the put-down may be true. Hurt is to a put-down what depression is to anger in general. In anger we hurl the threat back at its source. In hurt we turn the threat inward on ourselves. What is called hurt is a **mini-episode of depression.**

The very sensitive ego that needs good strokes from others in order to feel okay is most susceptible to hurt feelings. Diagram the following on the board.

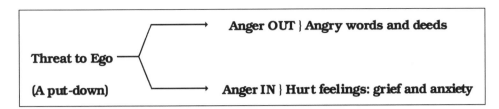

c. **The Third Anger Gremlin: Threats to Fairness**

Of all the threats that make Americans angry, threats to fairness stand at the front of the line. Welded as we are to a long tradition of democracy and fair play, even a minor threat to fairness is, for us, the *Great Gremlin.*

Put on the chalkboard, The Great Gremlin: Threats to Fairness. Most learners will need no more than that title to come up with a string of examples.

> **The Great Gremlin: Threats to Fairness**

(1) Civil Rights versus Uncivil Fights

Mix examples from their own lives such as, "I got grounded for a whole week. That wasn't fair!" with examples of inequality from society as a whole. All *deprivations of civil rights* are threats to fairness.

As with the other gremlins, we include actual, true deprivations of civil rights as well as intimidations and threats of potential deprivation. For as long as a genuine social inequality exists, it constitutes a continuing threat to fairness in the society as a whole. The real and present inequality is a threat in the sense that it is "an indication of something undesirable," something that, in itself, is "liable to bring danger."

Go over the examples of inequalities and unfairness listed on the board and ask, *"What emotion would you feel if this happened to you?"* Besides anger over the essential unfairness, note that in some cases the Great Gremlin arouses Gremlin 2, that is, continuing inequality produces a threat to ego, to self-esteem.

Sum up by stressing the common element to all three, that *ANGER IS THE NATURAL AND NORMAL REACTION TO THREAT.*

(2) Life Just IS

Finally, discuss with learners the saying, *"Life is neither fair nor unfair: It just IS."* Pass the wand to have each learner contribute. Explain that when we "take things personally," we fall into a common misunderstanding: that an oversupply of life's unfairness is intended just for us alone. Such a belief is prime garbage thinking. Most unfairness is not intended to single us out. Even when it does, self-pitying self-talk does nothing but make us unhappy and miserable.

ACTIVITIES

Choose one or a combination. Assign one for carryover.

1. **Journaling—Definitions**

   Instruct learners, *"Write in your journals definitions of threat, fact, belief, egotism, ego, Before Self-talk, After Self-talk, the two parts of anger, Help Talk, inequality, Gremlins 1 and 2, and The Great Gremlin."*

2. **Book Report**

   Assign learners to search the library for a biography of someone who was treated very unfairly. Have learners as individuals or in small groups give book reports. The reports should: (a) tell the person's story, and (b) detail the person's imaginary self-talk over the unfairness.

3. **My Personal Anger Management Plan, Part II**

   Instruct learners, *"We'll continue work on our Anger Management Plans. At the top of the second sheet write, 'My Special Gremlin'."* Write the title on the board.

   Instruct learners, *"Today we learned about Three Gremlins. Choose one that more particularly applies to you. That one is **your** Special Gremlin. Write two to three paragraphs (one page) in which you tell which one of the gremlins is your special gremlin and why. Be sure to give at least **two** examples from your life that show why that gremlin is indeed your Special Gremlin."*

   Most learners will choose Gremlin 2 or the Great Gremlin. Those who have experienced a real physical danger may choose to write about that experience. In this case one accident or incident of physical harm suffices. The goal is to personalize the lesson by having each learner relate the gremlins to personal life experience.

4. **"List of Anger Words," Activity Three**
   (Activity Sheet 5.1)

   Assign learners to write a story, "The Day I Turned Into a Tornado," using the List of Anger Words. Instruct that they use the words from the **third** column.

   Direct learners, *"Relate a story about a time when you were VERY angry, a time you were just furious. As you tell the story, do two things: first, use at least ten words from the third column of the List of Anger Words. Second, bring in the Gremlin that applies. For example, if you were furious because you felt you were being treated unfairly, bring the Great Gremlin into the tale."* As before, state your criteria for good English.

5. **Group Activity**
   "Action Plan For Challenges," (Activity Sheet 7.1)

Most protocols for problem solving fail in two respects. First, they set a poor tone by naming the issue a "problem." This immediately sets up the connotation of something burdensome, painful, and definitely not fun.

Secondly, typical problem-solving protocols fail to inquire about emotions. A situation is labeled a problem and yet the unspoken agreement is that no one, least of all the problem solvers, will talk about the emotions connected with and perhaps even creating the problem!

Resolve to eliminate the word, problem, from daily vocabulary for the word serves no constructive purpose. Other words such as challenge, issue, concern, and situation are much more amenable to positive, emotionally healthy handling. The directive, "Handle It!" is immensely more productive than, "Solve it."

The White House has a Situation Room, not a Problem Room! Use Activity Sheet 7.1 as appropriate throughout these lessons to constructively handle real-world situations. To begin, have learners identify a collective challenge. Work with them using this format as a guide to meeting the challenge.

BULLETIN BOARD MATERIAL

1. Life is neither fair nor unfair. It just IS.

2. Handle it!

Name: _____ Date: _____

Activity Sheet 7.1.

ACTION PLAN FOR CHALLENGES*

First, figure it out. Then, take constructive action.

FIGURING IT OUT

1. **What is my issue or concern?**

Before an issue or concern may be resolved, it must first be clearly identified. Tell about something of concern to you.

_____

_____

_____

_____

2. **How do I feel about it?**

Describe your emotions. How do you feel about the issue: mad? scared? sad? hurt? guilty? jealous? ashamed? or what?

_____

_____

_____

_____

3. **What is my self-talk about it?**

What do you say to yourself in your head about this concern? Do not write what you **think** about it but, what you really say to yourself, the actual words.

" _____

_____

_____

_____ "

---

*Sometimes called "PROBLEMS"!

*Permission granted to reproduce for classroom use. Taken from **Affective Self-Esteem** by Katherine Krefft, M.Ed., Ph.D. © 1993, Accelerated Development Inc., Publishers, 3808 W. Kilgore Avenue, Muncie, IN 47304-4896.*

Name: _____   Date: _____

⎡TAKING ACTION⎤

1. **How may I resolve it?**

   Think about the possibilities for resolving the issue. List as many ideas as possible. If you like, ask a friend to help.

   a. _____
   _____

   b. _____
   _____

   c. _____
   _____

   d. _____
   _____

   e. _____
   _____

   Use the reverse side of this sheet to list more ideas.

2. **Decide.**

   a.   Choose three ideas you think might resolve the issue.

   b.   Choose the idea you think will work best.

3. **How will I feel if I try this idea?**

   Describe the emotions you think you may feel.

   _____

   _____

4. **What self-talk will I use to help make my idea work?**

   What **new** self-talk is a more constructive way to handle this issue? Try self-talk that is the opposite of or different from your old self-talk.

   " _____
   _____ "

*Permission granted to reproduce for classroom use. Taken from **Affective Self-Esteem** by Katherine Krefft, M.Ed., Ph.D. © 1993, Accelerated Development Inc., Publishers, 3808 W. Kilgore Avenue, Muncie, IN 47304-4896.*

PHANTOM GREMLINS

OBJECTIVES

Learners will demonstrate their comprehension of

1. the differences and similarities between valid and invalid anger as demonstrated by oral and written exercises, and

2. their Anger Management Plan by adding examples of their own invalid angers.

MATERIALS

• Magic Wand

• Chalkboard or overhead projector

• A copy of the U.S. Constitution

• Drawing paper and red crayons or paint

• Magazine ads

• Journals for learners

• Activity Sheets 5.1, "List of Anger Words," and 7.1, "Action Plan For Challenges"

CONTENT

1. **Review**

   Collect carryover assignment. Review preceding lessons.

   • How does anger help us get what we need or want?

   • List some verbal and nonverbal ways we express anger.

   • List constructive ways to use the feeling part of anger.

- Name the two kinds of self-talk of the thinking part of anger.

- Describe Before Self-talk. Describe After Self-talk.

- What is a fact? What is a belief?

- Name three causes of anger, the Three Gremlins.

- Define threat and ego.

- Give examples of threats to self, ego, and fairness.

- What is the hurt of "hurt feelings?"

- Explain the difference between Anger In and Anger Out.

- Explain, *"Life is neither fair nor unfair. It just IS."*

- How have you used what you have learned?

2. **Valid and Invalid Anger**

This lesson extends and focuses the last lesson. Recall with learners that a threat is an intention to harm or an indication of something undesirable. Remind learners that a threat may be something regarded as liable to bring harm as well as that which is actually harmful.

In essence, then, a threat is internal self-talk along the line of, *"This is dangerous to me."* The **decision,** *"This is dangerous to me,"* may be **valid** and **real** or **invalid, not founded in reality—** a phantom.

As strange as it may sound, we frequently decide to view as harmful that which, objectively and rationally, is not dangerous. In this way we work up fear and anger over things that cannot really hurt us. But because we choose to believe in the danger, that BELIEF generates anger.

Explain to learners that when considering anger, our **beliefs** are the all important deciding factors. To discount a real danger is as damaging as to label as dangerous that which is harmless. In the first instance one sets oneself up to suffer real harm due to foolish disregard of the reality of danger. The second instance brings another type of foolishness. Unwarranted and disproportionate anger results from belief in the harmfulness of that which is not intrinsically harmful.

3. **Real and Phantom Gremlins**

Review with learners the first cause of anger as you put on the chalkboard, Gremlin 1: Threats to Self. Add two vertical columns for valid and invalid threats.

	Valid	Invalid
Gremlin 1: Threats to Self		

Review with learners that threats to self are threats of physical danger: threats, real or imagined, of actual physical harm. Continue, *"A **valid threat** is one that is real, actual, true—a threat that would be one to any other human being in the same circumstances. In this case the self-talk, 'This is dangerous,' reflects reality."*

a. **Phantom Poisons: Paranoia**

 *"But at other times we **imagine** that something is harmful or we uncritically accept an unfounded **belief** that something or someone or some group is harmful to us. This is an **invalid threat.***

 "For example, long ago people believed that tomatoes were poisonous. This belief was accepted and passed on for centuries. In Germany not until the end of the nineteenth century did people begin to eat tomatoes. Can you think of something else that was believed to be harmful and was later found to be perfectly safe? Or something thought safe that was later found to be harmful?"

 Another example learners will appreciate is the old belief that bathing frequently was not safe. Parallel with this was the firmly held belief that "invisible bugs" could not possibly cause disease. The nineteenth century genius, Dr. Louis Pasteur, suffered untold ridicule from one Dr. Charbonnet and the learned physicians of the French Academy for continuing to insist over many years that what was invisible could and did harm us.

 Fill in the chart with examples of valid and invalid threats to self. All **paranoia** and **imaginary harms** are examples of invalid threats to self.

b. **Threats to Ego**

 Continue the chart as follows.

THREATS

	Valid	Invalid
Gremlin 1: Threats to Self		
Gremlin 2: Threats to Ego		

Remind learners that Gremlin Number 2, the Ego Gremlin, is everywhere. Imagined threats to ego are frequent. For many people they are daily occurrences that generate as much anger as a slap in the face.

Imagined threats to ego are self-created. **Imagined threats to self-esteem and self-worth** are the put downs we put on ourselves. This process is sometimes called being too hard on yourself.

c. **The Wounded Ego Phantom**

For some, being wrong (about anything) is a massive **entirely self-created** put-down. The wounded ego syndrome is often a sign of invalid anger. Remind learners that by ego we mean that function in mind that tells us who we are and who we are not, our individual sense of self.

Thus, self-talk that limits and diminishes our sense of self is a put-down—but a **phantom** put-down. Such self-talk is real only as long as we believe it. It is real only *because* we believe it. It is real but invalid.

Though invalid, it creates real anger. A phantom may not be real, but if you think you see one, your fear is real enough. It is enough that the sojourn of life offers real humiliations to endure. We compound the challenge by inventing additional put-downs by our faulty beliefs.

d. **Threats to Fairness**

This is the Great Gremlin. Whereas deprivations of civil rights are examples of valid threats, imagined threats to fairness stem from **false appraisal of rights.** Anger due to a supposed lack of fairness is invalid when it stems from a belief that one has been deprived of something that is a right that, in actuality, is not.

Add the third section to the matrix and fill in.

THREATS

	Valid	Invalid
Gremlin 1: Threats to Self		
Gremlin 2: Threats to Ego		
Gremlin 3: Threats to Fairness		

e. **Phantom Rights**

Begin by distributing magazines and asking learners to find advertisements that appeal to them. Provide a copy of the Constitution. Explain that the Constitution is the proper source to consult for a listing of our rights as we understand them in the American community.

We confuse rights with privileges. By passing the wand, elicit from learners a list of **phantom rights,** those things that are believed to be rights but are not. For example, driving a car is a privilege, not a right.

As for "the right to be happy," a close reading shows that Jefferson was wise enough to promise us only the **pursuit** of happiness, not its final achievement. Much modern anger derives from our collective fantasy that life "is and by right ought to be" pain free and blissfully happy. Phantom rights create enormous anger.

Close scrutiny of advertisements and TV commercials reveals that many have the theme, *"You have a **right** to be happy, and so you **deserve** this product to **make** you happy."* Pass the wand to elicit examples from the magazine ads.

In particular, point to ads for alcohol and over-the-counter drugs. Also, ask for examples from television commercials. One of the saddest commentaries on today's society is the commercial that shows people drinking alcohol and explains, *"Life doesn't get any better than this!"* If the gusto of life is to be found in a can, the need for a War on Drugs is no surprise.

With examples offered by learners, demonstrate that commercials for over-the-counter drugs usually deliver the message, *"You have a **right** to be completely free from pain. Right now! So, if you have a pain, take a pill."*

Conclude by inviting learners to search the Constitution. Ask, *"Find where it says that happiness and freedom from pain are inalienable rights."* When we choose to imagine happiness is our constitutionally guaranteed right, we only guarantee ourselves angry constitutions.

ACTIVITIES

Choose one or a combination. Assign one for carryover.

1. **The Invention of Belief**

Assign learners to review history for examples of beliefs that were held true and subsequently proven or disproven. The history of invention is particularly instructive. Edison, for example, listened to many say that converting electricity into light was impossible. But because his **belief** was unshakable, we have the modern world we know.

2. **My Personal Anger Management Plan, Part III**

Instruct learners, *"We'll continue work on our personalized Anger Management Plans. On the third sheet write three examples of your own invalid anger and its phantom sources."* The three do not have to be one from each of the categories. They may repeat ideas from the last lesson which learners now realize are examples of **invalid** anger.

3. **"List of Anger Words," Activity Four (Activity Sheet 5.1)**

Assign learners to write a Whopper. Explain that before a Whopper was a hamburger, it was a tall tale full of exaggeration like the Paul Bunyan stories. Instruct learners to use as many synonyms for anger as possible. Direct them, *"Make up a story, a Whopper, a tall tale, about someone who showed all six kinds of anger. Use as many words in the List of Anger Words as you can. Be sure to bring in all three Gremlins."*

As before, state your requirements for good English. The goal is to highlight the ridiculous extent of our invalid angers.

4. **The Red Crayon Exercise**

Give all learners a red crayon and paper. Instruct them, *"You have ten minutes to draw a picture that shows the maddest you ever got."* After ten minutes, finished or not, collect, share, and discuss the pictures. **IMPORTANT:** Do **not** omit this final step of discussion. Be sure to resolve the anger to a comfortable level before finishing.

Pens and pencils also may be used to make the drawing, but the only color allowable is red. If facilities allow, interested learners may pursue the same activity with oil paints or water colors using only neutral tones and red.

5. **TV Homework**

Direct learners to watch TV for two hours. *"Write a summary of **every** commercial that has as its underlying message, 'This will make you happy' or 'You have a right to (= should have) this and what it will bring you.'"*

6. **Individual Activity "Action Plan for Challenges" (Activity Sheet 7.1)**

Direct learners to choose a personal challenge and use Activity Sheet 7.1 as a guide to handling it.

BULLETIN BOARD MATERIAL

America did not invent human rights. . . . Human rights invented America. Jimmy Carter

THE WIZARD'S BOXES

OBJECTIVES

Learners will demonstrate their comprehension of

1. the phantom expressions of anger and the meaning of forgiveness as manifested by listing their reactions to anger and by releasing anger, and

2. the differences and similarities among their own valid and invalid angers as demonstrated by completion of their Wizard's Boxes, a personal Anger Management Inventory.

MATERIALS

• Magic Wand

• Chalkboard or overhead projector

• A copy of the Constitution

• Circular papers and preparation for their disposal

• Activity Sheet 9.1, "My Wizard's Boxes"

CONTENT

1. **Review**

   Collect carryover assignment. Review last lesson.

   • What is a threat? How does it generate anger?

   • List some actual self-talk that indicates a belief that you are threatened by someone or something.

   • Describe some irrational beliefs about supposed threats that, objectively, are not threatening.

   • What is valid anger? Invalid anger?

- Describe the three gremlins of **_valid_** anger.

- Describe the three gremlins of **_invalid_** anger.

- Name three phantom gremlins.

- How have you used what you have learned?

- Close your eyes. What is on the bulletin board?

- Complete the following anger matrix. (Write the matrix on the board and work with learners to complete it.)

THREATS

	Valid	Invalid
Gremlin 1: Threats to Self		
Gremlin 2: Threats to Ego		
Gremlin 3: Threats to Fairness		

2. Phantom Solutions to Anger

Remind learners of the phantoms we discovered in the last lesson. Similarly, some ways of dealing with anger are mere phantom expressions. Explain to learners that **_revenge_** and **_hatred_** are forms of **_crystallized anger._** Many people today do not consciously connect acts of retribution with anger.

However, _"Don't get mad, get even,"_ is a classic piece of garbage thinking that clearly shows conversion of anger (a feeling) into revenge (an action). Revenge and hatred are simply phantom expressions of anger.

a. Adult Temper Tantrums

To yell, _"I hate you,"_ is not usually true hatred. It is a way of saying, _"I am mad as can be with you."_ If we were more honest, we would directly say, _"I'm furious!"_

However, taking **_hostile action_** out of anger is indeed hatred. Everyone acts aggressively sometimes. True hatred is hostile action taken with malice aforethought. Revenge and hatred are adult temper tantrums.

b. Stealing Power

Anger **_expands ego._** We sometimes choose revenge and hatred because they make ego feel large and powerful. The

actions taken allow us to move our limbs—as in the flailings of the two-year-old. These actions make us feel big and relieve the physical tension of the anger. *"Revenge is sweet"* because feeling powerful is sweet, that is, ego feels expansive and comfortable when acting with power, even illusory power.

Mature ego feels large enough without stealing power by hostility. Hatred and revenge are cheap ways to feel big. Infant egos feel bigger at the expense of others. Little egos step up by stepping on others.

Mature egos are confident enough in their own power that they refuse to steal it. They reject harming others in order to make themselves feel bigger. They may get just as angry as revengeful persons, but the difference is how they cross THE LINE. The difference is the **choices made.**

c. Forgiveness

To forgive is to release anger. To say, *"I forgive, but I won't forget,"* really means, *"Mentally, I forgive for that's what I've been taught, but I'm holding onto my anger."* It is emotion that makes us remember. *"I won't forget"* means *"I choose to hold onto my anger because not to do so is to experience my ego's smallness."*

True forgiveness comes only after feeling, expressing, and releasing the anger. Keeping hurts and angers as **secrets** maintains their emotional energy. Talking it out with someone, whether God or one of God's children, frees the emotions. Thus, releasing anger in forgiveness is not an altruistic act, a favor to the other person. Releasing anger heals one's *own* heart.

3. The Personal Anger Management Matrix

The class review matrix (in Item 1, above) completed on the chalkboard is a collective exercise intended to demonstrate the format for the individual work to follow. This individual task is the culmination of the preceding four lessons on anger. Abstract information about emotions is meaningless. Lessons on anger have been moving toward the exercise which is the heart of this lesson, a personal analysis of each learner's own valid and invalid threats to self, ego, and fairness.

After the class review and the presentation of Item 2, above, explain to learners that they are now ready to complete in their journals their own highly personalized Anger Management Matrix, an inventory of their own sources of anger and its expressions, phantom and otherwise. Explain that a matrix is a chart that arranges information in rows and columns.

a. **Enchanted Boxes**

Explain the purpose of the matrix as follows. *"Long before science took over the format, wizards like Merlin used 'magic boxes' to capture their wishes. To a wizard what was written was real. What was written in a box was as solid as stone.*

"So, we borrow enchantment from Merlin and use the matrix to help us look at ourselves objectively and clearly. By capturing our Magic Dragon in a matrix of boxes, we tame the dragon."

Distribute copies of Activity Sheet 9.1. Instruct each learner to work alone to complete the matrix. It may be made as detailed as possible within the time limits allowed. Since the charts by nature are very personal, assure learners that any sharing of them with the class shall be totally voluntary. However, see Activity 1, below, for an optional sharing technique. As learners are developing their charts, the teacher should circulate to offer individual assistance and support.

Instruct learners, *"Fill in each box in the matrix. For each threat listed make two entries: (1) the nature of the threat: What are the threats? and (2) the expression you apply to the anger: How do you react?"* List these two questions on the board. Learners are to list *as many* threats as they can think of, as many as apply. For, *"If you don't list it in the enchanted box, it will be very difficult for you to have power over it in the future."*

b. **Pointers**

Share with learners several pointers for completing a good matrix. First, stress the importance of **honesty.** To be honest about invalid threats is especially important. Now that learners realize such a thing as invalid threats do exist, they may hesitate to admit to having had beliefs they now realize are inaccurate. No one wants to admit he/she is wrong! Remind learners that when we uncritically accept an unfounded **belief** that something is harmful, that is an invalid, imaginary threat.

Second, remind learners that **imagined threats** to ego are frequent, daily occurrences. The daily ones are the self-created threats to self-esteem and self-worth, the put downs we put on ourselves. Ask learners to delve deeply into themselves to discover the ways in which they are too hard on themselves.

Third, urge learners to think about the **self-talk that limits** and diminishes their sense of self, their individuality. Remind learners that though this self-talk is in error, it creates real anger. Ask learners to thoughtfully examine whether, for them, being wrong is a key and crucial, self-created put-down.

Fourth, urge learners to be especially honest about what they believe to be **threats to fairness.** Young people are particularly apt to lament the unfairness of life. Point out, *"Life is neither fair nor unfair, it just is."* Remind learners that imagined threats to fairness result from a false appraisal of rights.

c. **The Fairness Boxes**

Only those who truly have been deprived of their constitutional rights, those who have suffered actual deprivation of civil rights, may validly make an entry in the Valid Threats to Fairness box. The teacher should not advise learners of this fact ahead of time. Simply allow learners to discover it for themselves.

Thus, as learners complete their charts, it will be helpful to have a copy of the U.S. Constitution in view. When learners puzzle over *"In what box do I put this?"* remind them that the Constitution alone states what are and, by omission, what are not our true rights. When learners debate whether a threat to fairness is "valid" or "invalid," do not explain more than the basic definitions.

For all questions of rights, invite learners to read the Constitution. They may be amazed to discover that very few will be able to list Valid Threats to Fairness.

Conversely, for many learners the box for Invalid Threats to Fairness—should we apply ruthless honesty—will be full to overflowing. Much contemporary anger is due to the false appraisal of supposed threats to fairness. Our collective American anger is not an appropriate response to objective, valid threats, but the inappropriate grumblings of egos that measure the world by the boundaries of self.

ACTIVITIES

Choose one or a combination. Assign one for carryover.

1. **Anger Management Partners**
   "My Wizard Boxes" (Activity Sheet 9.1)

   Encourage learners to find an anger management partner, a friend with whom they do not mind sharing their Wizard's Boxes. The role of the partner is two-fold: to give honest feedback on the chart and to serve as a sounding board with whom the partner may ventilate anger.

   Some learners may wish to choose the teacher or a school counselor as their anger management partner.

2. Anger Management Experts

Explain to learners that they are fast becoming anger management experts. An expert is a person with specialized knowledge in an area the majority know little about. The learners now possess specialized information about the nature and sources of anger.

Both to extend their own knowledge and to share it with others, learners may offer their expert services to others to develop anger management inventories. These may include: parents, teachers, principal, school staff members, brothers, sisters, friends, and students in other classes. Prizes and public recognition may be given to learners that bring to class an anger management matrix other than their own—with, of course, the permission of the person who received the expert assistance.

3. The Circle of Forgiveness Ceremony

Distribute papers in the shape of a circle. Explain, *"In your hands is a magic circle. On it write a brief description of something you've been very angry about. In particular name the person or persons at whom you are mad.*

"Since this is a magic circle, start writing around the outside of the circle. Move inward toward the middle writing around and around. What you leave in the middle is yours to keep. So as you get close to the middle, claim forgiveness with words like, 'I forgive Person X and release (her or him) into the Light' or to their Higher Power or into God's hands. Choose the wording you prefer."

Conclude the ceremony by burning the circles. As each one takes a turn, the learner may say, *"I release my anger and forgive."* If lighting a fire is not possible, the circles may be torn to confetti sized shreds.

NEW RIGHTS

A careful observer of American history will note that the progress of democracy is the centuries long process of defining new rights. Technically, the right to an education may not be in the Constitution, but today's laws affirm that every American has that right. But for how long? To age 16? Age 18? College? And what of medical care? Is it a right? For whom? Who has the right to which treatments?

Our consensus as to what is and is not a right evolves over time. Today's right was yesterday's privilege.

BULLETIN BOARD MATERIAL

1. Anger divides. Forgiveness heals.

2. Small people steal power. Big people share power.

3. Forgive and forget by releasing anger.

Name: _____   Date: _____

Activity Sheet 9.1
MY WIZARD'S BOXES

Each box is a category of threat that generates anger. Fill in as many items as you can in each box. For each box ask two questions: (1) What are the threats? (2) How do I react?

THREATS

	Valid	Invalid
Threats to Self		
Threats to Ego		
Threats to Fairness		

If necessary, use the back of the sheet, too.

Permission granted to reproduce for classroom use. Taken from **Affective Self-Esteem** *by Katherine Krefft, M.Ed., Ph.D.*
© *1993, Accelerated Development Inc., Publishers, 3808 W. Kilgore Avenue, Muncie, IN 47304-4896.*

WORD TRICKS

OBJECTIVES

Learners will demonstrate their comprehension of

1. their personal Anger Management Plan as shown by writing out coping strategies for valid and invalid anger, and

2. their ability to "handle it" as revealed by applying the Four Steps to incidents of anger.

MATERIALS

• Magic Wand

• Chalkboard or overhead projector

• Journals for learners

• Activity Sheet 10.1, "Should Inventory: Shoulds About Me"

CONTENT

1. **Review**

   Collect carryover assignment. Review last lesson.

   • Why are revenge and hatred phantom solutions to anger?

   • For whom do you forgive someone?

   • What is a matrix? How does it help us look at anger?

   • Ask learners who are willing to do so to share something new learned from their Wizard's Boxes, the anger matrix. What did you learn about your valid angers? Invalid angers?

   • Which area—threats to self, ego or fairness—give you the greatest challenge?

- What kind of self-talk leads us to work ourselves up into a good mad?

- We say, ***"He* or *she** makes me angry."* But really, who "makes" us angry?

- Is invalid anger weaker than valid anger?

- In our nation what document clearly states our rights?

- What have you believed to be a right that is not really a right? Would you add that right to the Constitution? Why or why not?

- How have you used what you have learned?

- Close your eyes. What is on the bulletin board?

2. Life Is Not a Problem to be Coped With

In the first lessons we discussed in general how to constructively handle emotions. Explain to learners that we avoid use of the phrase "to cope with emotions" as the word coping implies an ordeal. Emotions are not a horrible plague to be struggled through and "coped" with.

Stress to learners that emotions are part and parcel of our humanity. Our human emotionality is not a curse to be coped with but a gift that is taking us millennia to fully explore.

This is particularly true of anger. The phrases "to handle an emotion" and "to deal with it" are an improvement but not if "handling it" is construed as an enormous burden. "Handle it," "Deal with it," and "You can handle it" should imply, "You have the inner resources to handle it, so do so." Handling it always means ***constructively*** addressing and expressing the emotion.

3. Word Tricks: The Art of Handling It

Inner words that are powerful enough to create rage are truly magic. Remind learners that in these lessons we use magic as a theme because we, each of us, are like a magician. We have within ourselves the amazing power to find the inner words that—like magic!—will dispel the uncomfortable emotions our own words first created.

With our words, our faulty words, we trick ourselves into getting angry. So with our words we may trick ourselves out of the anger. Words, indeed, are magic. In this sense we could say that the following steps are all word tricks—but most powerful word tricks.

4. Handling It: The Four Steps

Explain that the purpose of the last several lessons has been to give learners tools to understand themselves and their emotions, anger in particular. The first step in handling it is to understand it.

a. **The Thinking Part of Handling It**

Write the following on the chalkboard.

> **STEPS IN HANDLING IT**
>
> **Step 1. Understand it.**

Pass the wand as you ask learners what they think "understand it" means. This is an opportunity to assess learners' level of comprehension of earlier lessons.

Then, explain, *"But understanding may be abstract, impersonal. Only a subjective approach yields the highly personal quality needed for truly handling it. That quality we name ruthless inner honesty."*

Write the following under step one.

> **Step 2. Apply ruthless inner honesty.**

Such honesty, by definition, is a challenge. Again pass the wand to solicit learners' input.

Then, sum up, *"Inner honesty is hard. It is supposed to be hard. If such honesty were easy, all humanity would have been saints ten thousand years ago. But each act of ruthless honesty is like a walk on the moon: one small step and one giant leap."*

The fruit of honesty and understanding should be action. If we understand and are honest but do nothing, we have only indulged in an academic exercise. Thus, the next step is an actual, tangible, concrete change.

> **Step 3. Change self-talk.**

In other words THE FIRST CHANGE MUST BE AN INNER CHANGE. To reduce anger and to handle any emotion we begin, always, within. We **shift focus** from what is happening "out there" to "make us angry" to what is happening within ourselves that is allowing the "out there" to have so much control over us.

Many ways of changing self-talk are possible. One good way to start is to examine the judgments we make about ourselves. Frequently, these judgments are self-statements using the word, "should." Add the following to step three.

Step 3. Change self-talk.
A. Eliminate self-judgments.

Other ways to modify self-talk are to use reminders and to eliminate garbage thinking.

B. Use self-reminders.
C. Pitch out garbage thinking.

A self-reminder is self-talk we choose to remind ourselves to change our thinking. Some examples follow.

- This is only my emotion-stimulated imagination.

- That's my fear talking.

- I'm angry. That's why I'm thinking these things.

- Mr. Hormone's got me again.

- I'm not really going crazy. It just feels like I am! I *can* handle it.

Pass the wand to elicit other examples from learners.

b. The Action Part of Handling It

At this point in our strategy we are ready to act on the emotion. The first three steps, understanding, honesty, and changing self-talk, are ***mental steps.***

But words are not, and will never be, feelings. We handle emotions by using our full humanity—our thinking AND our feeling. Steps one through three use thinking skills. The next step directly uses the emotions.

Step 4. Handle the emotion: Use the A, B, C's.

Refer back to Lesson Three to review the A, B, C's. They apply to all emotions. However, in this review stress their application to anger. Stop after reviewing the verbal channeling of the emotion. The nonverbal channeling of anger is the topic of the next lesson.

Leave the steps written on the chalkboard so that learners may proceed to Activity 1. As preparation for this task, ask for a volunteer to share a personal example of anger. Lead the class in a discussion that applies the Four Steps to that example.

Choose one or a combination. Assign one for carryover.

1. **Journaling—Handling It**

   Instruct learners, *"Review your anger inventory in your Wizard's Boxes* (Activity Sheet 9.1 of Lesson Nine). *Choose one example of valid anger and one of invalid anger and apply the Four Steps to state, step by step, how you will handle it in the future. Write your application of the Steps in your journals."*

2. **Handling It, Group Activity**

   If learners are not ready to work alone, divide them either into small groups or have them work with their anger management partner to, collectively, apply the Steps.

3. **Role-play**

   Ask for one volunteer to play Teacher and another to play Learner (or Student). Learner comes to Teacher with *"something that just happened that makes me angry."*

   Teacher leads Learner step by step through the Four Steps to handle it. If either gets stuck, they may ask for help from the audience. If time permits, do several performances and let learners vote for the Best Play.

4. **"Should Inventory: Shoulds about Me"**
   (Activity Sheet 10.1)

   Self-image consists of a string of self-statements about what one is and should be. When reality does not correspond with the inner self-talk, an emotional reaction is certain. When experience does not reflect our shoulds, we may feel any combination of guilt, shame, hurt, fear, disappointment, grief, and/or anger.

   Assign the worksheet and discuss with learners. Elicit insight into the connection between "shoulding ourselves" in self-judgments and emotions.

BULLETIN BOARD MATERIAL

   Ruthless inner honesty is
   One giant leap in one small step.

Name: _____   Date: _____

Activity Sheet 10.1
SHOULD INVENTORY: SHOULDS ABOUT ME

	MY SHOULDS	OTHERS' SHOULDS ABOUT ME
About my face	My face should look	Your face should look
About my body & weight	I should	You should
About my appearance	I should	You should
About my good points	I	You
About my weak points		
About my personality		
About me as female or male		
About my emotions		
About my intelligence		
About my talents and abilities		
About my future		

*Permission granted to reproduce for classroom use. Taken from **Affective Self-Esteem** by Katherine Krefft, M.Ed., Ph.D. © 1993, Accelerated Development Inc., Publishers, 3808 W. Kilgore Avenue, Muncie, IN 47304-4896.*

ILLUSIONS OF EGO

OBJECTIVES

Learners will demonstrate their comprehension of

1. the physical and emotional effects of anger as compared with other emotions as demonstrated by a self-analysis, and

2. their ability to Handle it! as evidenced by applying the full Four Steps to incidents of anger.

MATERIALS

- Magic Wand

- Chalkboard or overhead projector

- 3 x 5 cards

- Journals for learners

- Activity Sheet 11.1, "Should Inventory: Shoulds About Relationships"

CONTENT

1. **Review**

   Collect carryover assignment. Review the last lesson.

   - What do we mean when we say, Handle it?

   - List and describe the Four Steps of Handling It.

   - What is ruthless inner honesty? Why is it important?

   - Name three specific ways in which we may change our negative self-talk. Explain.

   - Complete: *"The first change must be . . . ."* Why?

- Describe the A, B, C's of constructive emotional expression as they apply to anger.

- Describe how *you* recently applied them to anger.

- How else have you used what you have learned?

- Close your eyes. What is on the bulletin board?

2. **Feelings in the Body**

Step 4 in the last lesson ended with the verbal channeling of emotions. Before we may fully understand how to nonverbally channel anger, we must first see how anger "sits" in the body. We have already learned that emotions are physical. One way to clarify what we are feeling emotionally is to investigate how the emotion "makes us feel" physically. List the following on the board.

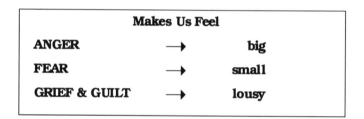

Makes Us Feel		
ANGER	→	big
FEAR	→	small
GRIEF & GUILT	→	lousy

a. **The Hot Air Illusion**

As you write the Makes Us Feel chart on the board, explain to learners that we choose anger over fear because, no matter how irrational the anger, it makes us feel bigger, more powerful.

Anger puffs out the ego. Inflated egos *feel* stronger, and that's why we keep inflating them. Alas, the inflation is an **illusion,** no more substantial than the air in a balloon. When push comes to shove, the balloon bursts. The chief recourse of the egoist is more hot air.

b. **The "Presto! No More Fear" Trick**

Yet still we choose anger over fear for fear makes us feel very small and helpless. When emotions are so strong that we crawl into bed and wither, crying, into **the fetal position,** we are feeling fear in all its painful purity.

Fear makes us feel so small that we retreat, even pulling our limbs closer to the body. Since fear feels so uncomfortable, we convert it into anger. We do so because we much prefer the feeling of power, even illusory power.

In this way, *"Anger is **a cover** for fear."* Anger is sometimes what it seems to be, anger, unalloyed rage. But frequently anger is a cop-out, a **mask for fear** or another uncomfortable emotion. Only ruthless inner honesty is able to sort out the difference between simple, honest anger and the stew of anger that is cooked up out of fear, grief, and guilt.

c. **Lousy Feelings**

Grief and guilt do not, so clearly, make us feel large or small. The word lousy seems to fit both. The lousy feeling of **grief** is an ache, a void, as expressed in the statement, *"When I lost him, I felt like my heart was cut out."* Grief is the **pain of loss** of an attachment.

The hurtful process of grieving has been amply and excellently described by Dr. Elisabeth Kubler-Ross. A loss, any loss, is like a death. The stages she described in her classic work, *On Death and Dying,*[3] define in detail the lousy feelings inherent in all grieving. Lessons Seventeen to Nineteen explore grief and related feelings.

Guilt seems to invoke the lousy feeling of **imagined nonexistence** as when we say, *"I feel so guilty, I could die."* The guilty frequently engage in self-sabotaging, self-damaging behavior. Guilt is the rejection of an erroneous behavior by rejecting self. The fundamental error is to **identify self with behavior,** *"I did bad. Therefore, I am bad."* Chronic guilt, then, is self-punishment based on this misunderstanding.

Guilt is the **failure of self-forgiveness.** It is the triumph of the ego that believes, *"I am too good to do bad."* Moderate guilt is a healthy prod to changing unacceptable behavior. But guilt that incapacitates and leads to self-sabotaging behavior such as substance abuse is wholly inappropriate. Lesson Twenty explores guilt.

d. **No Excuses**

As you outline the above to learners, pass the wand to obtain input. Stress that the lament, *"I don't know **what** I'm feeling!"* is no longer acceptable. For it IS always possible to know whether we are feeling large (that is, inflated), small, or lousy.

Learners may point out that fear, and sometimes anger, feel lousy, too. This is true. However, with just some practice most people learn to identify that unique, ego inflated, self-justifying, lousy feeling as anger and that particular, shrinking, lousy feeling as fear.

---

[3] Kubler-Ross, E. (1969). *On death and dying.* Toronto: Collier-Macmillan Canada.

3. **Locus Pocus**

As a final aid in identifying and expressing anger, we look at how anger "sits" in the body. "Locus" is Latin for "place." Diagram the following on the board.

Physical Locus of Anger		
LOCUS	**IMPULSE**	**REMEDY**
Upper body →	Fight →	Swing arms.
Lower body →	Flight →	Move legs.
Upper and lower →	Fight and flight →	Move arms and legs.

By understanding this model we may move to the final means of **constructive channeling** of anger, the **nonverbal.**

Remind learners that emotions are physiological, in the body. This physical reaction consisting of hormones and neurotransmitters is real and truly physical, not just "all in the mind."

a. **Use It Up**

For healthy emotional expression the physical discharge must be used up. It does not just instantly disappear because we say to ourselves, *"Calm down."* Now, *"Calm down"* is an excellent piece of self-talk. But when anger is intense, something more physical than speech is called for.

In today's world our most acceptable physical expression is called **exercise.** In short, sports and athletics in all its forms are our commonly accepted means of expressing intense physical energy.

b. **Work It Out**

Sports are sublimations of the Fight or Flight impulse. Pass the wand among learners as you complete the following chart on the board.

UPPER BODY "FIGHT" SPORTS	LOWER BODY "FLIGHT" SPORTS
Depend on	Depend on
Chest-shoulder-arm Power	Hip-leg-foot Power
Sports that primarily involve hitting and/or eye-hand coordination	Sports that primarily involve running and/or dexterity with the legs

Many sports involve both upper and lower body. In making the list center on the **primary** body emphasis. Tennis, for example, does involve running around the court, but hitting the ball is the primary focus of the game. To run a marathon is clearly lower body as is soccer. Swimming is both.

If learners differ on where they wish to place a sport, they may vote for the placement. The most important thing is not a precise listing but that learners see that we use sports to sublimate our Fight and Flight impulses.

c. **Identify Your Locus, Identify Your Sports**

Finally, personalize the exercise by having learners write in their journals a **list of sports** they prefer. They may make two lists, those they actually play and those they like to watch.

Continue the personal application by asking, *"When you get really, really angry, what do you do? Do you slam doors, throw things, or hit? Or do you run away by going for a walk or a drive? Or do you hit and then run?"* Have learners write in their journals whether their actions are primarily Upper Body or Lower Body expressions of anger.

If some learners appear stuck, prompt, *"Think of the time in your life you got the angriest. What did you do? Hit? Throw? Kick and stomp? If necessary, think back to what you did as a small child."* Some learners may require time to ask parents or relatives, *"When I was two years old, what did I do when I got mad?"* The inclination to be a hitter-thrower or a stomper-runner begins early.

Emphasize we place no moral judgment on running away as an expression of anger. Indeed, our genes are probably those of our ancestors who judiciously ran away from the saber tooth tiger, not of those who imprudently stayed to swing their arms and throw rocks.

ACTIVITIES

Choose one or a combination. Assign one for carryover.

1. **Anger Management Plan, Part IV**

Assign learners to complete the last segment of their Anger Management Plans. Remind them that in Lesson Eight they personalized their plans by writing three personal examples of their invalid anger. In Lesson Nine they completed an Anger Management Matrix and may have shared it with an Anger Management Partner. In Lesson Ten they applied the Four Steps of Handling It to their anger. The fourth step ended with the verbal expression of emotion.

Now it is time to consider the second part of Step 4, namely, the nonverbal (physical) expression of emotion. Direct learners to choose the mode of constructive physical expression they shall use as a safety-valve for explosive anger. Direct them to choose and list the sports, exercises, and other constructive activities (for example, gardening or cleaning out a room) that will be their chief physical means to use up and dispel anger.

Stress the importance of thinking through the possibilities and carefully choosing more than one activity. If one learner says, *"I'll take a walk,"* ask, *"Even if the weather is bad?"* If another says, *"I'll play tennis,"* ask, *"What if you can't find a partner?"* Guide learners to be realistic as well as specific.

An activity that may be pursued alone, such as running or, in bad weather, walking the mall several times, or hand ball, should be included along with activities requiring the participation of others.

2. The What If Game

Ask each learner to write out a What If situation on a 3 x 5 card. Each What If describes a difficult situation in which anger expression is a challenge. *"Think of a time you were angry about something or of a situation in which you might get very angry. Then, write a question describing the situation. Begin the question with the words, What if . . . ?"* For example, *"What if someone called you a stupid fool?"*

Collect and shuffle the cards. Have learners pull any card but their own and answer the question. Instruct learners that as they respond they are to follow what they have learned in this and prior lessons on anger management. Remind learners to include a physical activity or exercise as one of the steps in handling it.

As an aid, list the Four Steps of Handling It on the board before learners play the game. Accept silly answers and encourage laughter. At this point in our history appropriate responses to anger-provoking situations, *"I'd ignore him and walk away,"* are devalued and labeled "wimpish." Hostile reactions, *"I'd beat the hell out of him,"* are approved and applauded. Such is the overwhelming extent of our hunger for ego inflation.

Laughter deflates ego. With humor we relax and stop taking our egos so seriously. Humor refocuses our perspective, allows us to see our hostile urges in all their absurdity, and gives us precious time to stop and shift gears from raw emotion to logical thinking. Encourage learners to laugh at their extreme, aggressive "solutions" to What If. The more they laugh at such behaviors, the more likely they will not **act** on them.

3. **Sports ???**

Sometimes athletes directly express their anger. Lead learners in a discussion of sports figures who display or have displayed open anger. Ask learners, *"In your judgment is that a display of Upper Body or Lower Body anger? Does that anger help or hurt that player's game? If you were that athlete's trainer, how would you coach him or her to Handle It?"* Some learners may enjoy gathering pertinent articles from the sports pages and sports magazines.

4. **"Should Inventory: Shoulds about Relationships"**
   (Activity Sheet 11.1)

In addition to statements about what one should be, statements about relationships also contribute to self-image. When statements from self and others conflict, emotional reactions are common. When outer experience does not reflect the inner shoulds, then guilt, shame, hurt, fear, disappointment, grief, and anger may again plague us.

Assign the activity sheet and discuss with learners. Elicit insight into the connection between the "shoulding" of others and emotions.

BULLETIN BOARD MATERIAL

1.
Play out your anger
before your anger outplays you.

2.
Hit a ball, never a face.
Zap your gall: Run a race.

Name: _____   Date: _____

Activity Sheet 11.1
SHOULD INVENTORY:
SHOULDS ABOUT RELATIONSHIPS

	MY SHOULDS	OTHERS' SHOULDS ABOUT ME
About me as a son or daughter	I should	You should
About me as a sister or brother or family member	I	You
About me as a friend		
About me as a student and learner		
About me as a boyfriend or girlfriend		
About me as a team player or member of a class		
About me as a member of a community or church group		
About me as an American		

*Permission granted to reproduce for classroom use. Taken from **Affective Self-Esteem** by Katherine Krefft, M.Ed., Ph.D.
© 1993, Accelerated Development Inc., Publishers, 3808 W. Kilgore Avenue, Muncie, IN 47304-4896.*

UNIT III:
FEAR

GOBLINS, BOGEY MEN, AND LIES

OBJECTIVES

Learners will demonstrate their comprehension of

1. their understanding of fear as a emotion and how it works as revealed by sharing examples based on their new knowledge, and

2. the defense mechanisms of displacement, projection, and rationalization, and their relationship to societal prejudice as demonstrated by written and group activities.

MATERIALS

*   Magic Wand

*   Chalkboard or overhead projector

*   History books and/or newspapers

*   Journals for learners

*   Activity Sheet 12.1, "List of Fear Words"

CONTENT

1. **Review**

    Review the major concepts about anger taught in Lessons Five through Eleven. See previous review sections for appropriate questions. Collect carryover assignment.

    Then, review the last lesson as follows.

    *   How do the four challenging emotions feel in the body?

    *   Why do we choose anger over the other emotions?

- Explain, *"Anger is a cover for fear."*

- What would you say to someone who laments, *"I don't know what I'm feeling."*

- How does anger "sit" in the body?

- Place the following chart on the board and direct learners to complete it.

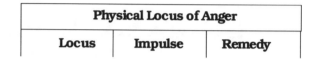

Physical Locus of Anger		
Locus	**Impulse**	**Remedy**

- Explain why and how intense anger must be expressed physically. (Relate responses to sports.)

- What physical activities or sports have you chosen to be part of your Anger Management Plan?

- How have you used what you have learned?

2. Introduction

Explain to learners, *"In studying anger we have already begun to study fear. In daily life fear and anger frequently happen together. In the next few lessons we shall examine and explore fear. We shall learn strategies for handling the bogey men and goblins of fear just as we've already learned to handle anger."*

Begin by asking learners, *"What have you learned about fear by studying anger? How are the two emotions the same? How are they different? Why do you think it may be helpful to study about fear?"* Pass the wand as you list responses on the board.

a. The Tough Guy Lie

One way to hook the interest of learners is to throw them a curve. Inform learners in a mildly teasing tone of voice, *"You guys need to study about fear, but I don't because I'm not afraid of anything!"* The claim *"I'm not afraid of anything!"* is frequently heard in movies, on TV, and from the mouths of macho teens. By adopting that same claim the teacher may effectively challenge it.

Playfully accept the learners' responses while yet insisting that *"Grown-ups aren't afraid of anything!"* Many adults indeed do have a mistaken belief that fear does not touch their lives. For some, alcohol and drug use masks the emotions to such an extent that the mistaken belief is easily maintained.

b. **Denial of Fear**

The ferocity of emotion with which the belief is insisted upon marks the intensity of denial of one's fears. Explore this notion with learners by moving progressively up the ladder of responsibility, authority, and privilege, *"Well, what about your parents? Are they ever afraid? What about the principal? Now there's someone who's never afraid of anything! No? Well, how about the mayor? The governor? The president?"*

Lead learners to discover, *"Everyone is afraid of something at some time."* Before we may get in touch with our fears, we must first have **permission** to do so. Talking frequently about emotions is the first step in making clear that everyone has them. Most people experience some measure of fear often. But because we as a society have an image of ourselves as fearless, we deny that fear.

3. Mind Tricks: Psychological Defense Mechanisms

Stress to learners that denying fear does not reduce it or make it go away. Denial of fear drives it underground. Then, it "comes out sideways" just as anger, too, can come out sideways.

Explain, *"The underground ways we have of taking care of emotions have names. **A defense mechanism** is a psychological process invented by our minds to attempt to protect us from uncomfortable emotions. A defense mechanism is a mind trick by which we try to fool ourselves that the emotion is not there or, if it is, that it does not mean what in our heart of hearts we know it means."*

Remind learners that in our first lessons we learned that emotions, although they are like water, do not evaporate. Instead, they build up until they are either expressed or expand the flood waters behind the dam. If such dams were perfect, we might be fine, although cut off from the wellspring of our emotions.

a. **Displacement: The Goblins**

But such dams inevitably leak. The emotion comes out sideways in a psychological defense mechanism known as **displacement.** Write the following on the board.

Displacement = emotions coming out sideways

Elicit examples from learners to demonstrate that displacement creates **goblins,** mischievous, ugly elves of our own design. Begin with the classic example of kicking the dog when you're mad at a person. Another well-known example is honking the horn at a stranger on the expressway when you are irritable.

The irritation may be the result of anger or fear or both or of another strong emotion. For example, creating a clique with tight membership rules is a displacement of one's own fear of not belonging.

Write examples on the chalkboard as learners pass the wand and offer other examples. Accept examples of displacement of anger as well as fear but ask, *"Which emotion do you think is coming out sideways here? Fear? Anger? Both?"* Add the following to the board.

> **Displacement = emotions coming out sideways = GOBLINS**

b. **Projection: The Bogey Man**

Explain to learners that an additional defense mechanism that is frequently used applies to fear as well as anger. Probably one of the most hurtful results of displacement of fear and anger is the further elaboration of the displacement process, *projection.* Write on the board

> **Projection = applying to another person feelings and beliefs within oneself**

Explain, *"Projection is denying one's own emotions by accusing someone else of those very same emotions! It is the defense of two-year-olds. 'I didn't do it. He did!' Seen this way, I think you'll agree with me that projection is cowardly and juvenile. Projection creates BOGEY MEN."*

Add "= BOGEY MEN" to the right of the definition of projection on the board. Pass the wand to elicit examples of projection from learners.

c. **The Biggest, Baddest Bogey Man**

The most notable manifestation of projection at work is *prejudice.* Thus continue, *"Whether it is prejudice against a certain race or ethnic group or against a clique of peers, the process is the same: one's own fear is projected outward in anger onto an identified group."* Diagram the process on the board.

> **Emotion → Denial → Displacement → Projection → Prejudice**

This cycle also may be diagrammed in a circular format.

Continue to explain, *"Extreme prejudice is called bigotry, intolerant zeal for an irrational opinion. The opinion is presented as a stubbornly held, fixed belief. But actually, the belief is thinly disguised **emotion** masquerading as an **idea.**

"Bigotry is always an emotional process. It denies and negates reason. Prejudice is a sign of emotions denied, displaced,*

projected, and generally run rampant. There's no such thing
as the Bogey Man, except the ones we ourselves create out
of our own fear and anger." And those are bogey men enough
for us to handle.

d. **Rationalization: The Big Lie**

On the board below the word, Prejudice, write, Reason.
Then mark through the word, Prejudice, with a prominent
X. Continue with, *"Prejudice is a sign of someone driven by*
their painful, uncomfortable emotions. **Bigotry** *is never a logical,*
rational decision, no matter how much we try to use logic to
defend it. Using logic to defend emotional decisions yields another
defense mechanism, one called rationalization." Write the following
on the board.

Rationalization = so-called logical excuse
for an emotion-based decision

Above the words displacement, projection, and rationalization
write in bold letters, DEFENSE MECHANISMS. To the right
of the definition of rationalization, write "= A LIE." Pass the
wand to elicit discussion of examples of rationalization, prejudice,
and other defenses.

4. **A Caution**

Be aware that individuals who are denying, displacing, and
projecting their emotions may not take kindly to being informed
of the fact. Expect strong reactions. If we were not afraid of
uncomfortable emotions, our minds would never have invented
these defenses in the first place. Some defenses are not intrinsically
"bad." For example, a person in the midst of an immediately life-
threatening event needs to deny the terror in order to have the
rational capacity to think clearly enough to attempt to survive.

But too often in daily life these defenses get out of hand and
produce inappropriate, unacceptable behavior. Societal prejudice
is a particularly ugly manifestation. Thus, discussion of personal
fears leads to discussion of society's fears. For in the prejudices
we live by—more strongly than by the ideals we verbalize—we
see the contradiction between the claim, *"I'm not afraid of anything!"*
and the actual world we have created.

ACTIVITIES

1. **Reason and Emotion in History**

With little difficulty one could demonstrate that human
history is the ages-long war between our collective denial,
displacement, projection, and rationalization and the enduring
force of human reason to combat those same emotional defenses.

Assign learners to find an event from history or current events that demonstrates the interplay of emotion and reason. First assign learners to work in small groups in class to complete the activity in a short class presentation. Then, assign learners to discover another such event and write the tale in their journals for a carryover activity.

Each version of the exercise should answer the questions, *"What emotions were at play? In your judgment what defense mechanisms were being used? Specifically, what was the role of fear? Of anger? Of other emotions? Where were the Goblins and Bogey men? Where was the voice of reason?"*

Often in history one key person is the voice of reason crying in the wilderness, e.g., Churchill in Britain just before World War II, Lincoln in his "bind up the wounds" speech as the Civil War was ending, Martin Luther King in his "I have a dream" speech, and so on.

2. "List of Fear Words," Activity One (Activity Sheet 12.1)

Assign an essay entitled something like "My Pet Anxiety" or "My Favorite Worry." Distribute the List of Fear Words and instruct learners to use only words from the *first* column. Other columns will be used later.

Ascribing human emotions to objects and animals generates insight, objectivity, and humor. In small groups learners may enjoy composing essays like "My Pet's Main Anxiety," "What an Orange Worries About," and "Insecurities of a Pen." Stories are to be written in first person as if the animal or object were telling the story.

3. Group Validation of Fears

Distribute five slips of paper to learners. Instruct them to write on each a description of something that frightens them. For more personal application direct that our collective fears of war, terrorism, global warming, etc., be set aside for this exercise. Instead let learners concentrate on their personal, daily fears.

Put all the slips of paper in a large container. As learners pull the slips one by one, discuss the general application of the fear listed. After the discussion, pin the slip to the bulletin board. Have the learners help arrange and rearrange the slips in order of priority from "Most Frightening" to "Least Frightening."

While the lessons on fear are being studied, the teacher may have one to three of these slips pulled a day. Learners share their input and then debate where the slip should go in the "Our Favorite Fears" listing. The daily process need take no more than five minutes.

Objectifying fear diffuses it. Putting a specific fear into a larger perspective often reduces its potency. As another variant, learners may vote for a "Fear of the Week," a specific fear all agree to work together to constructively address during that week. At the end of the week that slip may be posted under a heading, "Fears We've Conquered."

This exercise may require repeating two or more times. The first time around learners may be tentative about writing out their genuine fears. After additional study on emotions, learners may be more willing to risk sharing what really frightens them.

BULLETIN BOARD MATERIAL

1. Everyone's afraid of something some time. And that's okay.

2. Prejudice is fear projected outward in anger.

3. *Injustice anywhere is a threat to justice everywhere.*
   Martin Luther King, Jr.

Name: _____   Date: _____

Activity Sheet 12.1
LIST OF FEAR WORDS

Mild Fear	Moderate Fear	Intense Fear
shy	frightened	paralyzed
concerned	afraid	terrified
sheepish	scared	timid
nervous	anxious	panicky
tremulous	fidgety	shaky
solicitous	apprehensive	wary
shocked	numb with fear	scared to death
insecure	not confident	immobilized
alarmed	aghast	appalled
harrowing	dreadful	horrific
worried	fretful	fearful
startled	spooked	petrified
chicken	timorous	fainthearted
hesitant	reluctant	averse
loathsome	appalling	repulsive
sinister	ghastly	macabre
intimidating	threatening	menacing
foreboding	ominous	perilous
cowering	cringing	browbeaten
flinch	shrink	recoil
wince	quail	grovel
tremble	quiver	quake
horrified	dishearten	phobia
stupefy	trepidation	panic
dread	terror	suspicion
quaver	falter	tension
traumatic	cowardly	bashful
pusillanimous	lily-livered	defenseless

OTHER FEAR WORDS

_____   _____   _____

_____   _____   _____

_____   _____   _____

_____   _____   _____

*Permission granted to reproduce for classroom use. Taken from **Affective Self-Esteem** by Katherine Krefft, M.Ed., Ph.D. © 1993, Accelerated Development Inc., Publishers, 3808 W. Kilgore Avenue, Muncie, IN 47304-4896.*

PRESTO! ZAP YOUR PROBLEMS

OBJECTIVES

Learners will demonstrate their comprehension of

1. a broad definition of fear as evidenced by classroom discussion and written exercises,

2. valid and invalid fear as manifested by compiling a list of examples of the class' valid and invalid fears, and

3. a novel commitment to life without problems as proven by Taking the Pledge.

MATERIALS

- Magic Wand

- Chalkboard or overhead projector

- Journals for learners

- Activity Sheets 12.1, "List of Fear Words," and 13.1, "The Pledge"

CONTENT

1. **Review**

   Collect carryover assignment. Review the last lesson.

   - Give an example of an occasion when fear and anger occur together.

   - Did you ever know someone who claimed, *"I'm not afraid of anything!"*? What was he/she afraid of?

   - What happens to fear that is denied?

   - What is a psychological defense mechanism?

- What is displacement? How does it create Goblins?

- Give an example of displacement.

- What is projection? How does it create the Bogey Man?

- Give an example of projection.

- What is one of the most notable manifestations in society of the process of projection?

- Diagram the cycle that leads from emotion to prejudice.

- What defense mechanism comes under the disguise of a logical excuse? Give an example.

- To sum up, what are Goblins, the Bogey Man, and Lies?

- How have you used what you have learned?

- Close your eyes. What is on the bulletin board?

2. **Fear Defined**

Begin with, *"Since we've been talking about fear, we need a clear definition. What is fear?"* Accept learners' responses, and write them on the board. Someone may look the word up in the dictionary. However, following is a **definition** very helpful to learning how to handle fear. At the appropriate time add the following definition to the board.

> **Fear is the natural and normal human response to danger and the unknown.**

Then, explain the definition phrase by phrase as follows.

a. **Fear Is Normal. Macho Is Not**

We emphasize that fear is *"natural and normal"* because so many people believe *"something's wrong **with me"*** when they are afraid. Those who believe they are not afraid of anything mistakenly believe that they are **abnormal,** a **failure,** or a **coward** when they feel fear.

Popular **media** advances this belief. The Duke, Rocky, and Rambo in their many incarnations all support the false belief, *"If you're afraid, there is something wrong with you. If you're afraid, you're something less than a man, even less than human."* The "something wrong" is usually expressed in ugly, derogatory, demeaning language. To make the point, pass the wand to elicit from learners the common slang synonyms for coward (wimp, sissy, etc.) with which they are well familiar.

b.   **Fear Is Human. Macho Is . . . ?**

Similarly, we stress that fear is "human." From our observations of animals it appears that they, too, feel fear. We cannot know with absolute assurance that **animals experience fear** in just the same way humans do. Do animals have a thinking part of fear or only a feeling part? We do know that fearful behavior has been observed in animals. From this we **intuit** that animals feel fear.

Perhaps because we observe animals sometimes behaving fearfully, we may easily conclude that fear is an animal response and, thus, something less than human. But a trait shared by all humanity in all ages is clearly a **human** quality. To reinforce that fear is human, not less than human, our definition calls it a "human" response.

c.   **Danger and the Unknown**

Fear is the response to danger and the unknown. Explain to learners that like all emotions fear has a thinking part and a feeling part. The **thinking part** consists of the perception of self as diminished, small, and weak. Such a state constitutes a "danger."

The **feeling part** consists of uncomfortable, "gut level," internal sensations, and physiological alterations in the body. The next lesson looks at this part of fear.

3. **The Lions' Cage**

Fundamentally, the thinking part is **self-talk,** conscious or subconscious, which says, *"This is dangerous to me."* One may be in a situation which **objectively** is dangerous, even potentially lethal, and not feel fear if one does not interpret the situation as dangerous.

For example, a lion tamer is an expert animal trainer. However, a lions' cage is, objectively, a very dangerous situation. In it the trainer relies on knowledge and skill for safety. Either the lion tamer does not feel fear at all or, feeling it, suppresses it until out of the cage. Animal experts know that lions seem to smell fear. The trainer handles fear constructively in order to safely exit the cage.

Conversely, one may be in a situation that **objectively** is not at all dangerous but be very fearful because the situation is construed to be dangerous. For example, fear of rejection, real or imagined, by a peer group is a "danger" that is a potent producer of anxiety.

The teenage prom is not nearly as dangerous as the lions' cage. But it may be terrifying. Who will go with me? Will I look all right? Who will dance with me? What if I trip in the middle of the dance floor? What if my face breaks out the night before the prom? What if my parents don't let me stay out as late as the other kids?

4. **The Great Unknown**

We respond with fear to the unknown when we suspect danger in that unknown. Facing the unknown may also generate feelings of *expectation, adventure,* and *delight.*

As an example, share with learners what we know about one of the greatest explorations of the unknown of all time. Columbus felt expectation and excitement at his great adventure. But as the weeks dragged on, his sailors descended from apprehension to fear to sheer terror. Columbus must have felt moments of fear, not from falling off the world, but from mutiny. But his faith in the correctness of his knowledge and in his own leadership skills enabled him to continuously focus on the adventure of his exploit, not on his fear.

Columbus' example reveals that when the mind views new challenges only as dangerous obstacles and fearful burdens, then *fear replaces anticipation.* For this reason eliminating *the word, problem,* and substituting instead words like challenge, obstacle, issue, and concern are advisable. This is the way to zap your problems—like magic!

Danger and the unknown produce lack of certainty and the absence of surety. The state of not feeling secure or safe is called *insecurity.* The absence of assured safety and predictable certainty is very anxiety provoking.

For children lack of consistency in parenting and irregular, erratic discipline create intense fearfulness. When the self-talk is, *"What will happen next, and how will I survive it?"*, the prospect of both danger and the unknown produces fear that may mount to terror.

5. **Valid and Invalid Fear**

Just as sources of anger are valid and invalid, sources of fear also are valid and invalid. A *valid danger,* one that is objectively real, produces *valid fear.* Even so, like the lion tamer one may condition oneself to reject or bypass fear. Write the following on the board.

> **Valid danger → Valid fear**

But so-called dangers, things that would not generate fear in most people most of the time, things that are not inherently dangerous, are *invalid dangers.* They generate real but *invalid fear.* Add the following to the board.

> **Invalid danger → Invalid fear**

Stress again that this fear, although objectively invalid, is quite real.

With the category of the unknown we cannot make exactly the same equation. Things are either **known** or **unknown.** If something is but partially known, one is fearful of that portion that remains unknown. Thus, "invalid unknowns" cannot exist. If it is not unknown, it must be known. If a known object or situation generates fear, it must be because it is perceived as dangerous.

Thus, complete the chart on the board.

Unknowns → Valid Fears

ACTIVITIES

1. **Taking "The Pledge," A Class Exercise**
   (Activity Sheet 13.1)

   Instruct learners to each take out a sheet of paper and their journals. Direct them to use the sheet to write a "List of My Problems." The list may be as long or short as time allows.

   Then, working as a class or in small groups, have learners reframe each "problem." Direct them to rewrite them in their journals in terms of a challenge, obstacle, issue, or concern, or synonyms to these words. For example, *"Talking to my parents is my biggest problem"* is reframed in the journal as, *"Talking to my parents is my greatest challenge."* Instruct learners to choose a title for this journal page.

   Upon completion of the exercise, invite learners to "throw their problems away" by crumbling or tearing the single sheet titled "List of My Problems" and discarding it in a trash can. Then, with due ceremony, have each learner Take the Pledge by solemnly reading and signing their own copy of the Pledge (Activity Sheet 13.1).

   Note that even when we throw away our problems, life's challenges remain.

2. **Valid and Invalid Fears**

   Assign learners to make two lists in their journals: one, a List of Valid Fears, those that are appropriate responses to valid, real-world dangers; and two, a List of Invalid Fears, those that are inappropriate responses or overreactions to that which is not objectively dangerous.

   At the beginning of the next class have learners share their lists. The process should generate discussion and even debate because of possible differences of opinion about what is and what is not objectively dangerous. The point is not to generate debate to the death over *"Is this a valid or invalid fear?"* but to inculcate these key concepts: (1) not all fears are valid, and (2) it is perfectly acceptable to experience fear in fear-provoking circumstances.

3. **"List of Fear Words," Activity Two (Activity Sheet 12.1)**

Assign learners to use the List of Fear Words, column two, to write a story, "A Scary Day." Instruct them to mainly use words from column two. A few words may come from column one. Save column three for next lesson's exercise. Instruct them to tell the story of an average day they found frightening. This is *not* a tale of terror but of an ordinary, everyday fear that, one day, was particularly anxiety-provoking.

BULLETIN BOARD MATERIAL

1. I have many challenges and some obstacles, issues, and concerns—but no problems.

2. Every life challenge is an exciting discovery!

Activity Sheet 13.1
THE PLEDGE

I hereby state, declare, and affirm that henceforth in my life and for all time to come I shall have

NO PROBLEMS.

However, I reserve the right to have

- Issues to attend to,

- Concerns to handle,

- Obstacles to overcome, and

- Challenges to grapple with.

Duly signed and sealed this day,

_____

[Date]

By: _____

[Name of no-problem person]

_____

[Name of witness]

*Permission granted to reproduce for classroom use. Taken from **Affective Self-Esteem** by Katherine Krefft, M.Ed., Ph.D. © 1993, Accelerated Development Inc., Publishers, 3808 W. Kilgore Avenue, Muncie, IN 47304-4896.*

MYSTIC DEWDROPS

OBJECTIVES

Learners will demonstrate their comprehension of

1. the feeling part of fear and constructive conflict resolution as demonstrated by class discussion and written exercises;

2. the significance of their own valid fears and strategies for handling them as evidenced by applying to them the A, B, C's of constructive emotional expression; and

3. the meaning and importance of crying as the primary nonverbal means of emotional expression as manifested by class discussion and an exercise with a hand mirror.

MATERIALS

- Magic Wand

- Chalkboard or overhead projector

- Small hand mirror

- Journals for learners

- Activity Sheets 12.1, "List of Fear Words"; 14.1, "Win-Win Conflict Resolution. With Emotion!"; and 14.2, "Win-Win Conflict Resolution. With Emotion, Worksheet One"

CONTENT

1. **Review**

    Collect carryover assignment. Review the last lesson.

    - Define fear.

    - Why do we say fear is natural and normal?

- Why do we say that fear is a human response?

- What is the thinking part of fear?

- Give an example of fear that is a response to a valid danger. To an invalid danger.

- When is an unknown fearful?

- Describe other feelings the unknown may generate.

- Why do we take the pledge and drop the word, problem, from our vocabulary?

- Of what does insecurity consist?

- How have you used what you have learned?

2. **The Feeling Part of Fear**

In the last two lessons we learned about the thinking part of fear. This lesson and the next one focus on the feeling part of fear and allow learners to more fully explore their own fears. Additionally, in this lesson the teacher has the option of beginning instruction in a step by step *affective* conflict resolution process.

Remind learners that we have seen that emotions are physiological and mental. The mental or thinking part is entirely different from the physiological, feeling part.

3. **The Physical Fear Reaction**

Once fear is elicited one may say over and over, *"I'm not afraid,"* but the pumping heart, altered breathing, and other physical reactions like a dry throat together loudly proclaim, *"You ARE afraid."* To elicit more symptoms of fear, ask, *"What do we mean by 'gut-level' fear?"*

The *fear reaction* is a complex physiological process which includes the release of *hormones* into the bloodstream and changes in *neurotransmitters* in the brain. Once fear has progressed to this point, the statement, *"It's all in your mind,"* simply is not true. It's in your body.

Remind learners of all they have learned about the need to find a *physical outlet* to express potent emotion. An Affective Management Plan is a way to handle all strong emotions, in particular, the most challenging ones, fear, grief, and anger.

Thus, at this point instruct learners to review their Anger Management Plans and see what portions of it also may apply to other strong emotions. Pass the wand and elicit input on strategies for handling fear and grief.

a. **Allowing Fear**

The review may, in part, anticipate some of the following. Lead learners in a discussion to remind them of what they have learned about the A, B, C's of constructive emotional expression. Now apply the A, B, C's to fear. Write the following on the board.

A. ALLOW the emotion.

Then, follow an outline of questions similar to these.

- How do we know when we're afraid?

- Do we always know when we're afraid?

- If we feel big or inflated when we're mad, how do we feel when we're afraid?

- What kind of self-talk occurs when we're afraid?

- If we fail to *own* the fear, what happens to it?

- Could we express the fear as something else?

- What self-talk might we use to label fear?

- What effect does drinking alcohol and getting high have on Step A?

- "Tough guys" get in fights all the time. Of what are they afraid?

Honest and **direct self-talk** is best. *"I'm afraid. I wish I were not afraid, but I have to admit the truth is I really am scared."* In the discussion lead learners to see that the first step in handling fear is to name the emotion correctly, to admit that it is what it is, and to claim it as one's own. Erase the word, emotion, and write, fear. Add the following sentences.

**A. ALLOW the fear. Allow it to happen.
Claim it. Own it. Name it.**

---

b. **Feeling Fear**

Ask learners if they recall Step B. If necessary, write a hint on the board.

B. BE

Then, complete the statement as you lead a discussion on how to apply Step B to fear.

B. BE WITH the emotion.

- **What do we mean when we say *be with* fear?**

- If we run away from our fears, what happens?

- Do they just go away, poof?

- What are some *direct* ways we may express fear?

- How do alcohol and drugs interfere with Step B?

- What happens when the drug wears off or you sober up? Is the emotion still there?

Remind learners that to be with an emotion is to feel it and experience it directly, honestly. When we fail to do so, the emotion comes out sideways in some alternate, usually inappropriate expression. Emotions never just evaporate, poof. They find an outlet whether or not we consciously direct the process.

Add the following to the board.

B. BE WITH the fear. FEEL it. AND:

Then, continue, *"And what? What is nature's main, physical outlet for fear?"*

Screaming is certainly one such outlet. But if learners do not at first see that *crying* is nature's main, physical outlet for fear, point to the openings for the lacrimal glands in the inner corner of your eyes. Ask, *"Why do we all have these two, tiny holes?"*

4. The Lost Art of Crying

Indeed, crying is the natural outlet for all strong emotion, joy as well as anger, sorrow, and fear. But in our day the subject of crying is a sensitive one, more particularly so for boys and men. The American culture is chock full of *"Don't cry"* signals.

Little boys, more often than girls, are told, *"Don't cry."* A young boy who cries is called a crybaby. A youngster who expresses fear is labeled a scaredy cat. Rough, tough motion picture heros are hardly ever seen to cry. The message communicated and internalized as self-talk is, *"If I am to be a real man, I must not cry."*

Garbage thinking does not stop being junk just because it is embraced by mass culture. But by living on top of the garbage dump, one does get used to the smell. Thus, it takes stepping back and applying ruthless inner honesty and critical thinking to reject the garbage thinking advocated by society.

Lead learners in a discussion of the objective purpose of tears, our mystic dewdrops. Lead them to an understanding that in a society that degrades crying, a real man is the man who dares to cry. It takes no courage to follow the crowd. Daring to go it alone by expressing your true feelings takes intrepid valor.

5. **Laughing Through Tears**

Exaggeration and teasing are good techniques to diffuse fears of a sensitive subject. For youngsters that are highly resistant to hearing the message, *"It's okay to cry,"* point to each facial feature one by one and ask its purpose. Follow an outline similar to the one below.

- Point to your mouth. *"What do we do with this?"* (We eat. We talk.) *"Is it okay to eat and talk?"* (Yes.) *"Then, it's not unmanly or childish to eat and talk?"* (No.) *"It doesn't make me a little kid if I eat and talk?"* (No.)

- Point to your nose. *"What is this thing that sticks out of your face for?"* (To smell, to breathe.) *"Is it okay to smell and breathe?"* (Of course.) *"So, a real man does not have to hold his breath, does he?"* (No.)

- Point to your eyes. *"What are these two blue or brown or green things for?"* (To see.) Close your eyes. *"Suppose someone tells me a real man or a real woman walks around with his or her eyes shut like this. Then do I have to close my eyes all the time to be real?"* (No.) *"No! Why not? You have to admit it would take a really tough guy to do that. So why not?"*

- Lightly pull your earlobes. *"What are these flappy things for?"* (To help us hear.) *"Well, what if a bunch of people decide to paint their earlobes green and then say, 'You're not grown up until your ears are green.' Would you paint your ears?"* (Various responses are to be expected.) *"Why or why not?"*

- Pass around a small mirror. *"Okay, I want all of you to check your faces. Is anyone missing a mouth? Nose? Eyes? Ears?"*

- *"Now! examine the inside corner of your lower eyelids carefully. Does anyone **not** have the tiny holes that are the openings of the lacrimal glands? Are they present in only the girls?"*

- *"What are they for?"* (Crying.) *"Are they for anything else?"* (To wash the eyes as when your eyes "water.") *"Well, your nose is for two things, too, smelling and breathing. Suppose that an evil witch put a spell on you so that from now on you could only do **one** of those. Which one would it be? Your mouth is for two things, too, eating and talking. But that busy witch says you have to choose one. What is your choice? How much fun would life be without talking and the sense of smell?"*

- *"So, here we have holes in our lower eyelids that are meant for two things. But some of us listen to that stingy ole witch who says we may only use them for **one** thing. Our lacrimal ducts are for crying, so is it okay to use them?"*

NOTE: If there is a handicapped individual present, modify the above exercise as sensitivity and decorum suggest.

In bold letters add the word CRY behind the AND in Step B. Sum up by reemphasizing that crying, in fact, is the natural outlet for all strong emotion

ACTIVITIES

1. **"List of Fear Words," Activity Three (Activity Sheet 12.1)**

    Instruct learners, *"Invent a fantasy story about an imagined day of terror that is horrifically funny. Call it something like 'The Silliest Day of Terror'."* Direct them to use as many words as they can from column three of Activity Sheet 12.1, the "List of Fear Words." Similes and metaphors also may be used, for example, *"I was as scared as a . . ."* or *"My fear was a torrent of black pitch choking my breath away."*

    Encourage them also to use exaggeration and absurdity. The fantasy is not to be a copy of movie and TV horror scripts. It may be a **satire,** a mock and silly imitation of one such plot. Or it may be entirely original.

    Humor diffuses anxiety. Humor reduces the dangerous to manageable proportions. Humor mocks our fear of the unknown by creating something, if only a thread, we may handle. When we turn ignorance to humor, the familiarity of that humor comforts us and dissipates the fear.

2. **A Nightmare on [Your Street]**

    Assign learners to work together in small groups to invent a nightmare. First, learners compose the scripts. Then, they act them as plays.

    However, as in Activity 1 unlike the usual blood and gore horror movie, these plays are to be blood free—no guns, knives, chain saws, etc. Rather, learners must concoct "Something Terrible" that is not murderously violent. For example, "My Dog and the Monster Flea." Dialogue of characters should include words from Activity Sheet 12.1, the "List of Fear Words," all three columns.

3. **Mystic Dewdrops**

    Instruct learners, *"Write a poem about magical, mystical, enchanted tears that are as precious as diamonds and pearls.*

Whose tears are they? Why are they magic? What wonderful feats of wizardry do they work?"

4. **"Win-Win Conflict Resolution. With Emotion"!**
   (Activity Sheets 14.1 through 16.2)

   As with "problem" solving, most conflict resolution protocols totally ignore emotion. When negotiators cannot agree on the shape of the negotiating table, it is not logic but emotion that is primary. When emotion is ignored, non-issues are treated as if they were substantive. Attention is deflected from true issues.

   Only after hours of verbalizing and ventilating have relieved the emotion do negotiators get down to business. But detailed, multi-page documents are poor substitutes for direct, constructive anxiety and anger expression. Activity Sheets 14.1 through 16.2 offer a protocol for negotiating based on affective as well as cognitive input.

The Art of Crying

Many people are afraid to cry for two reasons: one, they are afraid to have others see them, and two, they are afraid they will not be able to stop crying once they start. The solution is to cry in the shower. Being alone in the bathroom resolves the first concern. The flow of water from the shower resolves the second. For one cannot cry and put one's face under the stream of water at the same time. Invite learners to try it.

BULLETIN BOARD MATERIAL

1. It's okay to be afraid.

2. No feelings are bad. Some actions are.

Name: _____   Date: _____

Activity Sheet 14.1
WIN-WIN CONFLICT RESOLUTION.
WITH EMOTION!

BEGINNING

To begin, each disputant agrees to become a **Negotiator.** A neutral third party accepts the role of **Diplomat,** a referee.

DUTIES OF THE TWO NEGOTIATORS

- To be honest and open

- To listen

- To talk about emotions as well as ideas

- To give a little, to bend

- To commit to a win-win solution

DUTIES OF THE DIPLOMAT

- To be fair and impartial

- To listen

- To clarify emotions by reflecting what both negotiators say

- To guide the conflict to a win-win situation

Specific time limits are agreed upon for each of the steps.

STEP ONE   Time limit: _____ minutes

The Diplomat directs each Negotiator, *"Describe the matter as you see it."* In the process complete Worksheet One.

- In reference to this matter I feel . . . .

- In reference to this matter I want . . . .

- In reference to this matter I need . . . .

- In reference to this matter I would like . . . .

- In reference to this matter I wish . . . .

Negotiators share their worksheets for the specific, prearranged time limit. In this step each Negotiator speaks directly to the Diplomat while the other Negotiator LISTENS IN SILENCE.

*Permission granted to reproduce for classroom use. Taken from **Affective Self-Esteem** by Katherine Krefft, M.Ed., Ph.D. © 1993, Accelerated Development Inc., Publishers, 3808 W. Kilgore Avenue, Muncie, IN 47304-4896.*

Name: _____ Date: _____

Activity Sheet 14.2
WIN-WIN CONFLICT RESOLUTION. WITH EMOTION!
Worksheet One

- In reference to this matter I feel . . . .

  _____

  _____

- In reference to this matter I want . . . .

  _____

  _____

- In reference to this matter I need . . . .

  _____

  _____

- In reference to this matter I would like . . . .

  _____

  _____

- In reference to this matter I wish . . . .

  _____

  _____

- Additionally, I want to say . . . .

  _____

  _____

  _____

  _____

Remember! While sharing this worksheet, the Negotiator speaks directly to the Diplomat while the other Negotiator LISTENS IN SILENCE.

*Permission granted to reproduce for classroom use. Taken from **Affective Self-Esteem** by Katherine Krefft, M.Ed., Ph.D. © 1993, Accelerated Development Inc., Publishers, 3808 W. Kilgore Avenue, Muncie, IN 47304-4896.*

CONSTRUCTIVE FEAR

OBJECTIVES

Learners will demonstrate their comprehension of

1. more strategies to handle fear as manifested by class discussion and written exercises, and

2. the significance of their valid fears and the strategies for handling them as demonstrated by applying the A, B, C's of constructive emotional expression and win-win conflict resolution.

MATERIALS

• Magic Wand

• Chalkboard or overhead projector

• Journals for learners

• Activity Sheets 12.1, "List of Fear Words," and 15.1, "Win-Win Conflict Resolution. With Emotion! Worksheet Two"

CONTENT

1. **Review**

   Collect carryover assignment. Review the last lesson.

   • Describe the feeling part of fear.

   • If someone told you fear was "all in your mind," what would you say?

   • Name the first two steps in the constructive emotional expression of fear.

   • What does Step A, "Allow the fear," mean?

   • What does Step B, "Be with the fear," mean?

- (Point to your lacrimal ducts.) What is the purpose of these two holes? Is it okay to use them?

- What would you say to someone who insisted, *"A real man (or woman) doesn't cry"*?

- What do drugs like alcohol and marijuana do to emotions?

- How have you used what you have learned?

- Close your eyes. What is on the bulletin board?

2. **Step C**

   Begin by reminding learners, *"In our last lesson we learned to apply Steps A and B to fear. Today we're going to see how to apply Step C also."* Write steps A and B on the board.

   > **Step A. Allow the fear. Allow it to happen.**
   > **Step B. Be with the fear. Feel it.**

   "Who remembers Step C?" Add the following.

   > **Step C. CHANNEL the emotion.**

   We may express fear in two major ways, verbally and nonverbally. **Talk it out!** is the first and foremost way to verbally express fear. Nonverbal expressions include art, music, and physical exercise that works off the physiological emotional discharge.

   Erase the word, emotion, from Step C on the board and substitute the word, fear. Begin to list the various constructive strategies for fear.

   > **Step C. CHANNEL the fear.**
   >
   > • **Talk it out!**

   a. **Emotions Are Energy**

      Remind learners that emotions are energy to be used to make things happen. The energy of emotion may be directed to constructive purposes. Even fear, as uncomfortable as it is, may be channeled into productive ends.

   b. **Fear Is A Prod To Action**

      Explain to learners, *"Fear, like anger, can be a powerful motivator. For example, if you are afraid you are going to fail, you just might study harder. If you are scared no one will like you, you might try harder to be a nice person. If you are afraid the police are going to catch you, you might not drink and drive. Mild fear is an important prod to action. In fact, many daily actions are motivated by a moderate level of fear."*

3. **Channeling Fear**

As each category of constructive channeling is discussed, add it to the board.

> **Step C. CHANNEL the fear.**
>
> - **Talk it out!**
> - **Change your self-talk.**
> - **Seek new knowledge.**
> - **Ask for help.**
> - **Ask for a hug.**
> - **Take constructive action.**
> - **Practice courage!**

a. **Change Self-talk**

Explain to learners, *"The key to constructively handling fear is your self-talk. Isn't that interesting? The key to doing a good job of handling the feeling part of fear is **changing** the thinking part! Once those hormones are in your bloodstream, you can't poof! them away like magic. BUT you may always, always **change your thinking.** You can change your self-talk. You can learn to talk yourself through your fear and come out on top!"*

Ask learners, *"What are some **new forms of self-talk** you may use when you're thinking, 'This is scary'?"* Pass the wand as you list on the board learners' suggestions such as, *"It's scary, but I can handle it,"* and *"It's as exciting as it is scary,"* and *"It's not so scary when I think, 'I can do it. Other people have. So can I.' "*

b. **Seek New Knowledge**

When fear is the fear of the unknown, the obvious solution is to **eliminate the unknown factor.** New information may come from reading, from talking to others, from watching a pertinent video or film, and from experience. To learn not to be afraid of something means to see that something in a new, non-dangerous light.

Encourage learners, *"When you are afraid, ask yourself, 'Am I scared because I'm seeing this as new, strange, uncertain, unknown? Is it something I've never dealt with?' If so, then the next question is, 'Where or to whom may I turn to get the information I need to help me deal with this?' After that, it's a matter of taking action, of actually applying the information obtained."*

c. **Ask For Help**

Many people have the mistaken idea that needing help with something, with anything, means that they are weak or unmanly or less than perfect. All human beings are growing. Therefore, **all human beings are imperfect.** To objectively view a situation and decide that one is over one's head takes courage.

To ask for help, therefore, is a act of wisdom that demonstrates true **strength of character.** By failing to ask for help when reason suggests we need help, we often scare ourselves far beyond the situation warrants. We perpetuate and deepen our pain and anxiety.

Explain to learners, *"There is nothing shameful in admitting that something we see as dangerous or frightening or new is scaring us. But to pretend, to 'fake,' knowledge and abilities that we do not have but could have if we just asked for help— that is the true shame. Ask for help. It won't kill you. But acting out of your fear just might."*

Self-help and **twelve step groups** such as AA have expanded the helping principle to the organizational level. When common challenges are shared, the fear, too, is shared and thereby reduced. Fear thrives in secrecy and silence.

d. **Ask For A Hug**

When fear is very strong, seeking knowledge and practicing new self-talk and all such rational approaches are very difficult. Please note. They are not **impossible.** They are **difficult.** If one has a belief that one should be exempt from doing hard things, these options may **feel** impossible. Today many have a belief that life "should" be easy and that, if it is not, something is wrong.

As you explain this, in bold letters write the following key self-talk on the board.

LIFE IS SUPPOSED TO BE HARD.

Make clear the following, *"I said life is supposed to be hard, not overwhelming or impossible, just hard. Just hard enough to keep us reaching, to keep us trying, to keep us growing. When life is hard and a little scary, nothing is 'wrong.'*

*"When life is hard and scary, we scare ourselves even more when our self-talk tells us, 'Something is wrong.' We have to turn that around and say, 'Nothing is wrong. This is hard and a little scary for me, that's all. **I can still be okay** when things are hard and scary. I need some hugs, and I'm going to ask for them.'"*

When fear is prominent, **nurturance** has no substitute. Everyone has had the experience of seeing a fearful child calm down in the arms of a loving parent. When fear refuses to give way to reason, the human touch—a hug, a kiss, an arm around a shoulder, a pat on the hand—works miracles. Nurturance, if not a cure, is a sure treatment for fear. It often reduces fear "like magic."

People caught in tragic, fatal situations such as a plane going down, a cave-in, or lost at sea, instinctively reach out for a human touch. Holding a human hand will not abort the tragedy, but it does help us face something as scary as death with just a little less fear. If this is true in the face of death, how much more so for all daily fears! Give hugs freely. Ask for hugs often.

e. **Take Constructive Action**

Changing self-talk, seeking knowledge, and asking for help or a hug are all forms of constructive action. However, **other forms of action** may be helpful or necessary. For example, if the source of fear is objective danger, the solution is to remove or avoid the danger. If one is afraid of the dark, light is the simplest solution. If one is afraid of an abusive boyfriend or girlfriend, the time may have come to dissolve the relationship.

Explain, "**Not deciding IS deciding.** *To allow ourselves to be paralyzed by fear is to choose to sink deeper and deeper into that fear. Sometimes it is best to do something rather than nothing. When we have asked for help and obtained all the information we can, it's time to fish or cut bait. Act. Do something, but act.*

"*It's true at times we have to be patient and wait a very long time for what we want, but we want the **waiting** to be an **active choice.** Even waiting may be a constructive action if we're clear that waiting is the choice we're making. **Patience** is not passive endurance. Patience is a decision to hold off on something for the present because we see that if we do so, there's a better something in the future.*"

In situations in which immediate action would not be productive an **indirect action** that expresses the fear is helpful. Art, music, and constructive physical activity all serve to channel fear. Selections of Wagner's music and Picasso's art incarnate fear in sound, form, and color.

f. **Practice Courage!**

Explain to learners that the final strategy for handling fear is something called courage. Courage is so important that it is a lesson unto itself.

1. **"List of Fear Words," Activity Four**
   (Activity Sheet 12.1)

   Instruct learners to use whatever words they choose from all three columns of Activity Sheet 12.1 to describe an event or something in their lives they find or once found frightening. This is a serious essay to be titled something like, "What Scares Me" or "What Scared Me." By now learners should be familiar with the range of intensity expressed in the three columns. Instruct them that the purpose of this activity is to choose their words carefully to express just the exact quality of fear that best describes their feelings.

   Learners may write a paragraph or story as you direct. Advise them whether or not the writings will be read in class as this may influence the choice of topic.

2. **A Nightmare**

   Encourage learners to write or tell an actual nightmare dreamed either recently or when younger. Other class members then share their input as to what they think the dream may mean. The intent of this activity is not to play amateur psychologist but to give learners' new knowledge about fear ample field for expression.

   A nightmare, by definition, is a frightening dream. Learners will enjoy trying to decipher the specific nature of the fear in a given dream. Learners will come away from the exercise understanding that "it's only a dream" is not a sufficient explanation. It's fear, too.

3. **Journaling—What I Will Do**

   Direct learners, *"Write in your journals a list of your fears, valid and invalid. After each fear, skip three or four lines."* Then continue, *"Now go back and under each fear write the things you intend to do in the future when you experience that fear."*

   As in other lessons, if learners find it very difficult to work alone, have them complete the exercise in small groups.

4. **"Win-Win Conflict Resolution. With Emotion"!**
   (Activity Sheet 15.1)

   Continue with the conflict resolution exercise. In this portion use Activity Sheet 15.1 to clarify the points on which the negotiating parties agree and disagree. This concludes Steps One and Two.

The activity sheets at the end of the next lesson detail **NOTES** Step Three and the final step.

BULLETIN BOARD MATERIAL

1. Life is sometimes hard. But I can handle it!

2. When I'm afraid, I will: Talk it out! Change my self-talk. Seek knowledge. Ask for help and a hug. Take constructive action. Practice courage!

Name: _____ Date: _____

Activity Sheet 15.1
WIN-WIN CONFLICT RESOLUTION. WITH EMOTION!
Worksheet Two

Time limit: ___ minutes

The Diplomat assists the Negotiators in writing out an Agree/Disagree List. Don't forget to include in the listing **emotions** shared in common. For example, "*We're both angry,*" and "*We're both afraid.*" Negotiators may speak directly to each other as well as directly to the Diplomat.

POINTS ON WHICH WE AGREE	POINTS ON WHICH WE DISAGREE
1. _____	1. _____
2. _____	2. _____
3. _____	3. _____
4. _____	4. _____
5. _____	5. _____
6. _____	6. _____
7. _____	7. _____

*Permission granted to reproduce for classroom use. Taken from **Affective Self-Esteem** by Katherine Krefft, M.Ed., Ph.D. © 1993, Accelerated Development Inc., Publishers, 3808 W. Kilgore Avenue, Muncie, IN 47304-4896.*

COURAGE!

OBJECTIVES

Learners will demonstrate their comprehension of

1. additional strategies for handling fear as evidenced by class discussion and individual exercises, and

2. a new definition of courage as illustrated by exercises that require application of that definition.

MATERIALS

• Magic Wand

• Chalkboard or overhead projector

• An unabridged dictionary

• Copies of *Huckleberry Finn* and *Profiles in Courage*

• Journals for learners

• Activity Sheets 12.1, "List of Fear Words"; 16.1, "Win-Win Conflict Resolution. With Emotion! Page Two"; and 16.2, "Win-Win Conflict Resolution. With Emotion! Worksheet Three"

CONTENT

1. **Review**

   Collect carryover assignment. Review the last lesson.

   • Name the A, B, C's of constructive fear expression.

   • How may a moderate level of fear be helpful?

   • Name several constructive ways to channel fear.

   • Can we talk our fear away? What part of fear can we talk away, the feeling part or the thinking part?

- List some anti-fear self-talk.

- What is the solution to fear of the unknown?

- Name two ways of getting new information.

- If someone said, *"Only wimps need to ask for help,"* what would you say to contest that view?

- If we need help and don't ask for it, how are we hurting ourselves?

- When fear is very strong, what is the "cure"?

- Is life supposed to be easy? Why or why not?

- When life is hard and scary, how do we scare ourselves even further? What self-talk scares us further?

- Besides asking for help, what else may we ask for?

- Besides a hug, what other kinds of nurturance help us feel less afraid?

- What do we mean when we say, "Take constructive action"?

- Explain why not deciding IS deciding.

- What is patience? What is it good for?

- How have you used what you have learned?

2. **Courage Is More Than Intestinal Fortitude**

   Explain to learners that fear is an opportunity to develop strength and courage. Since we are all born as babies, we are all crybabies. **Crying** is one of our first acts as independent human beings. Crying comes first, and courage follows close behind.

   No one grows up without repeatedly facing fearful situations and learning to handle them. **Facing fear** teaches us that it is not so bad as we feared. We can handle it. What frightens us most may be just the experience we need in order to learn that we are strong enough to face our worst fears.

   a. **Courage Is Action**

   Write the following on the board with the definition of courage in bold letters.

   > **Step C. Channel the fear.**
   >
   > **COURAGE IS BEING AFRAID OF TAKING CONSTRUCTIVE ACTION AND DOING SO ANYWAY.**

Explain to learners, "Courage **is not** the absence of fear. Courage is feeling fear and **acting in spite of** that fear. It is a grave mistake to assume that brave people do not feel afraid. A prevalent, popular misunderstanding of the meaning of courage is that it means to be fearless, that is, to be without fear.

"But not to be afraid in an objectively fear-provoking situation is either, (1) foolish, or (2) superhuman. None of us are superhuman. Folly does nothing to maximize human potential. Fear is the natural and normal human response to danger and the unknown.

"Fear does not make one a coward. **Lack of action** does. Courage is being afraid of doing what you know you must and doing it anyway. Courage is a decision to act. Courage is **a decision, not a feeling.** Courage seldom feels good when you are in the act of practicing it. The fear does not go away just because you have decided to act in spite of it. In fact, it may increase. But later, perhaps many years later, you may look back on the incident with deep satisfaction.

"To act with courage and experience yourself as strong enough to face fear produces a feeling of **self-competence** like no other. Human fulfillment is the fruit of fears successfully faced year after year. If a hero is someone who acts with courage, then we are all heros."

b. **Everyday Courage**

Pass the wand to elicit from learners examples of the many, small acts of courage that fill our days. Begin with the fact that sometimes getting out of bed in the morning is an act of courage. Talking politely to someone you fear does not like you takes pluck. Smiling at someone who never smiles back is an act of valor. Trying to do, again, something you have failed at before takes bold resolve. Working to change a habitual behavior that you know is in your best interest to change takes true grit.

As the wand circulates, write the following title on the board.

ACTS OF COURAGE

Under the title write learners' suggestions as they are made. In the discussion teach the following **synonyms for courage:** bravery, valor, mettle, pluck, spunk, and gumption. Add synonyms for the adjective, courageous: dauntless, intrepid, bold, valiant, and stouthearted. Invite learners to use one of the synonyms to describe the act of courage as it is added to the list on the board.

An unabridged dictionary will assist in defining the subtle shades of difference in the synonyms. Adding popular slang equivalents for courage is at the teacher's option.

3. **Two Americans of Courage**

Americans like to think of themselves as fearless. We mistake fearlessness for courage. In fact, as the preceding activity may have revealed, some dictionaries list fearless as a synonym for courage. But since strictly speaking "fear-less" means "without fear," it cannot also mean courageous. Courage is *not* foolhardiness, fearlessness, and daring which are the reckless, brazen acts of the daredevil. Mark Twain understood this.

a. **A Courageous Writer**

Twain was an American of great courage. Today, we take his faith in the equality of all persons for granted. Staunchly, he wrote his beliefs into his works thereby shocking prim society and getting *Huckleberry Finn* (1884) banned in Boston.

Twain understood the subtle difference between mock fearlessness and true courage. Ask learners to listen as you read the following from Mark Twain. Pause at the slash (/).

Courage observes;/ reflects; calculates; surveys the whole situation;/ counts the cost, estimates the odds, makes up its mind;/ then goes at the enterprise resolute to win or perish./ Recklessness does not reflect,/ it plunges fearlessly in with a hurrah,/ and takes the risks, whatever they may be,/ regardless of expense. [4]

Instruct learners to open their journals. Direct them, *"At the top of a sheet write the word, 'Courage,' and under it write what you think Mark Twain said about it. In the middle of the sheet write the word, 'Recklessness,' and under it write what he said about it. Do you want me to read the passage again?"*

Undoubtedly, the response will be yes. Read slowly but do not write the quotation out. The idea is for learners to listen carefully and write in their own words what they think Twain is saying. After no more than three readings, compare and contrast interpretations.

b. **A Courageous President**

John F. Kennedy, our 35th President, wrote *Profiles in Courage.*[5] Give learners a brief synopsis of his life. Then, lead a discussion around questions such as these: *"What did he do that showed courage? Do you think he was ever afraid?*

---

[4] Twain, M. (1907). *Christian science* (p. 154). New York: Harper & Brothers.

[5] Kennedy, J.F. (1964). *Profiles in courage.* (Memorial Edition, pp. 259, 264-265, 266). New York: Harper & Row.

When? Do you think there was a time he let fear get the better of him? When or how? Was there a time he was reckless?" There was. He once crashed a PT boat into a pier.

Some intriguing anecdotal evidence suggests that the President was warned not to go to Dallas. Conclude this portion of the discussion by inquiring, *"Suppose President Kennedy had been warned that his life would be in danger if he went to Dallas. If so, why did he go?"*

As with the quotation from Mark Twain, read the following quotations from *Profiles in Courage*. Ask learners to write in their journals what they think the passages mean. Read each excerpt up to three times. Have learners write, then discuss. Read one or more.

Excerpt 1

It is when the politician / loves neither the public good nor himself,/ or when his love for himself is limited/ and is satisfied by the trappings of office,/ that the public interest is badly served./ And it is when his regard for himself is so high/ that his own self-respect demands he follow the path of courage and conscience/ that all benefit.

Excerpt 2

The true democracy . . . puts its faith in the people/ . . . faith that the people/ will not condemn those whose devotion to principle leads them to unpopular courses,/ but will reward courage, respect honor and ultimately recognize right./ . . . For, in a democracy, every citizen, regardless of his interest in politics,/ "holds office";/ every one of us is in a position of responsibility;/ and, in the final analysis, the kind of government we get/ depends upon how we fulfill those responsibilities./ We, the people, are the boss,/ and we will get the kind of political leadership, be it good or bad,/ that we demand and deserve.

Excerpt 3

The courage of life/ is often a less dramatic spectacle than the courage of a final moment;/ but it is no less a magnificent mixture of triumph and tragedy./ A man does what he must—in spite of personal consequences,/ in spite of obstacles and dangers and pressures—/and that is the basis of all human morality.

ACTIVITIES

1. **"List of Fear Words," Activity Five**
   (Activity Sheet 12.1)

   Instruct learners to refer to the List of Fear Words as they write an essay, "The Bravest Thing I Ever Did," on a time they acted with courage.

2. **Literary Adventures**

   • *Huckleberry Finn*

   Direct learners to read or review the book. Write an essay that answers these questions: *"Whom do you think is the most courageous character in the book? Taking Mark Twain's own definition of courage, show point by point how that character was courageous. Was that character ever reckless? Using Mark Twain's definition, show how that character was or was not reckless."* Share with learners a typed copy of the quotation from Mark Twain.

   • *Profiles In Courage*

   Instruct learners to read a chapter from the book. Direct, *"Choose one of President Kennedy's profiles of John Quincy Adams, Daniel Webster, Thomas Hart Benton, Sam Houston, Bob Taft, or one of the other American heroes. Using Mark Twain's definitions and President Kennedy's words, show why you think that person was a courageous American."* Make copies of the quotations available.

3. **Journaling—Popular Sayings**

   Direct learners to explain in their journals what the following sayings mean.

   • Discretion is the better part of valor.

   • *The only thing we have to fear is fear itself.* (Franklin Roosevelt)

   • . . . to boldly go where no one has gone before.

4. **"Win-Win Conflict Resolution. With Emotion"!**
   (Activity Sheets 16.1 and 16.2)

   Continue and conclude the exercise by working through Steps Three and Four.

BULLETIN BOARD MATERIAL

1. Courage is being afraid of taking constructive action and doing so anyway.

2. *A man does what he must—in spite of personal consequences, in spite of obstacles and dangers and pressures—and that is the basis of all human morality.*

   John F. Kennedy

3. Sometimes just living is an act of courage.

Name: _____ Date: _____

Activity Sheet 16.1
WIN-WIN CONFLICT RESOLUTION.
WITH EMOTION!

STEP THREE   Time limit: _____ minutes

The Diplomat assists the Negotiators in writing out a list of all solutions that may apply. Freely list all solutions that come to mind on the sheet marked, "List of Possible Solutions."

Phase One. Negotiators offer solutions from their own points of view.

Phase Two. The Diplomat directs each Negotiator to switch chairs. Now each Negotiator must pretend to be the other person and offer solutions from that person's point of view.

In talking about solutions consider also the **consequences** and **impact** of each potential solution.

STEP FOUR   Time limit: _____ minutes

The Diplomat directs each Negotiator to speak directly to each other as they use a process of elimination to come up with the chosen solution. Negotiators work as follows.

- Negotiators MUTUALLY AGREE on eliminating from the List the *two* potential solutions that are most unacceptable to both of them.

- Negotiators MUTUALLY AGREE on eliminating the next two least acceptable solutions.

- Negotiators continue in this manner until a solution acceptable to both is reached.

The Diplomat's job here is to remind Negotiators to speak directly to one another and to continue to talk about emotions. After a solution is reached, the Diplomat concludes negotiations by summarizing the agreement and asking each Negotiator, *"What are your emotions upon reaching this solution?"* Negotiators may sign a contract affirming the agreement.

With mutual agreement the negotiations may be extended to include more participants. Each Negotiator may have an Assistant Negotiator to serve as a helper. When Negotiators switch chairs, so do their Assistants. The Diplomat may have one or more Consultants to assist in referee duties. A number of Observers may be appointed to listen in silence and afterwards evaluate how well each participant accomplished each role.

*Permission granted to reproduce for classroom use. Taken from **Affective Self-Esteem** by Katherine Krefft, M.Ed., Ph.D. © 1993, Accelerated Development Inc., Publishers, 3808 W. Kilgore Avenue, Muncie, IN 47304-4896.*

Name: _____   Date: _____

Activity Sheet 16.2
WIN-WIN CONFLICT RESOLUTION.
WITH EMOTION!
Worksheet Three

List of Possible Solutions

Use the reverse side to list additional solutions.

1. _____
   _____
   _____

2. _____
   _____
   _____

3. _____
   _____
   _____

4. _____
   _____
   _____

5. _____
   _____
   _____

6. _____
   _____
   _____

7. _____
   _____
   _____

8. _____
   _____
   _____

*Permission granted to reproduce for classroom use. Taken from **Affective Self-Esteem** by Katherine Krefft, M.Ed., Ph.D.*
© 1993, Accelerated Development Inc., Publishers, 3808 W. Kilgore Avenue, Muncie, IN 47304-4896.

UNIT IV:
GRIEF

THE MISTS OF GRIEF

OBJECTIVES

Learners will demonstrate their comprehension of

1. the nature of attachment, loss, and valid and invalid grief as manifested by the sharing of personal examples in class discussion and written exercises; and

2. the stages of grief defined by Dr. Elisabeth Kubler-Ross as shown by applying them to a personal life experience.

MATERIALS

- Magic Wand

- Chalkboard or overhead projector

- Journals for learners

- Activity Sheet 17.1, "List of Feeling Words"

CONTENT

1. **Review**

   Collect carryover assignment. Review the last lesson.

   - What is good about fear?

   - What is courage?

   - Describe a fearless person. Describe a courageous person.

   - What makes a person a coward?

   - Does courage feel good? When?

   - Why are we all heros?

- Describe two acts of courage.

- Name some other words for courage.

- Name two Americans who showed courage.

- What did Mark Twain say was the difference between courage and recklessness?

- What president wrote which book about courage?

- How did President Kennedy define self-respect?

- What did President Kennedy mean when he said
    —that in a democracy the people reward courage?
    —that every citizen holds office?
    —that we get the leadership, good or bad, that we demand and deserve?

- What did President Kennedy say was less dramatic but no less magnificent than the courage of a final moment?

- What did President Kennedy say was the basis of all human morality?

- How have you used what you have learned?

- Close your eyes. What is on the bulletin board?

2. **When The Sunshine Dies**

The process of creating and severing bonds is the cycle of life. If emotions in general are like water, then grief is like a mist. Sometimes it may be like a soft morning mist that shrouds the landscape at dawn. But frequently, it is like a thick fog that envelops all things.

Grief is a veil that neutralizes the color of life. It is a murky haze that makes seeing where one is and where one is going very difficult. Often it feels like a heavy mantle that makes the simplest movement an act of enormous courage.

Explain to learners that grief is the **natural and normal** human **response to loss.** With society's elimination of mourning rituals many people do not know the natural cycle of grief. Like all emotions, grief comes in a flow that peaks and recedes in crests and troughs. The pain of grief alternates with quieter moments. As time passes, the peaks of the crests become less high. The length of time in the ebb stage increases.

With the passing years the length of time in the ebb stage exceeds that of the crests of pain. Yet when attachment has been great, the pain felt on the anniversary of a death may mirror the original. Fear, anger, and guilt are emotions that may be completely worked through and released. But grief for the loss of a great love may be carried until one's own death.

a. **Grief Defined**

Grief is sorrowful **sadness** that results from the **severing** of a bond of **attachment.** We cannot lose that to which we are not attached. Thus, for grief to be felt a process of **identification** must first occur. One's self-identity must be somehow viewed as tied into the other person, place, or thing.

As you lead learners in a discussion of attachment, loss, invalid grief, and the stages of grief, pass the wand to elicit input from learners' personal experiences. Be sensitive to their reactions, especially to individuals who suddenly fall silent or avert their gaze from you. These may be learners who have been particularly touched by loss. Be alert to signs in classroom reactions and in the activities that may warrant referrals to school counselors and/or psychologists.

b. **Attachment and Loss**

Many types of loss exist. The object of potential loss may be a person, a family member, friend, or loved one. It may be a popular figure that one does not personally know. Pass the wand as you ask learners to give examples of types of loss they have experienced.

Then explain that loss may even be of oneself in the form of loss of self-esteem or a habitual form of self-expression. **Loss of self,** even when the habits given up are self-destructive, may produce profound grief. The object also may be a loved pet, a favorite object, or a cherished place like a home.

As with other emotions grief may be valid or invalid. Valid loss produces valid grief. In **valid grief** the object of the loss was first appropriately or reasonably identified with ego. The object was defined or seen as a part of self *and also* as a separate individual. **Healthy attachment** respects the other person and accepts that person as a fully separate individual. The key to healthy attachment is balance, proportion, and maturity based on genuine respect for the other's independence.

Unhealthy attachment sees the other only as an extension of self. Seeing the choices of the other person only or primarily in reference to self produces **dependency,** not valid relationship. **Emotional enmeshment,** not love, results when two people expect each other to meet all their emotional needs. Americans understand political independence. Few understand emotional independence.

3. Forms of Invalid Grief

Invalid grief, then, is genuine and real but invalid because it is based on invalid premises. Invalid loss produces invalid grief. Invalid grief is based on **misidentification,** namely, something is identified as a "loss" that one never possessed in the first place.

a. **Jealousy**

Jealousy is a form of **fear,** not love. Possessiveness is motivated by fear of one's own loss, not by regard for the other person. The 1989 movie, *Fatal Attraction,* gives a clear depiction of the extremes of the process. Pass the wand to elicit from learners other examples from popular media and personal experiences.

Use these examples to point out that when one overidentifies with another person, loss of that other is felt as a loss of self. Ask learners, *"What have we discovered happens when the self is threatened?"* Anger happens. Thus, possessiveness produces jealous rages.

Invalid expectations also may produce invalid grief. This process occurs when we expect the attachment to do something that attachments by nature cannot do. The attachment does not live up to our **erroneous beliefs.** As a result, we grieve. The lyrics of many popular songs reflect our many, collective, mistaken expectations about relationships. For example, one song moans, *"I've got to know if your sweet love is going to save me."* The song has it backward. If anything saves us, it is the process of loving—of love freely given.

b. **Love and Attachment**

Mature attachment, then, is based on acceptance of the **essential aloneness** of the human condition. First, we accept the self as necessarily solitary and independent. Second, we respect others: their independence, their feelings, their choices. Third, from two separate selves we create love. From childhood to adolescence to adulthood we grow in understanding the meaning of mature attachment. Then, when we grieve, it is valid, not invalid, grief.

4. The Stages of Grief

Dr. Elisabeth Kubler-Ross in her book *On Death and Dying* (Toronto: Collier-Macmillan Canada Ltd., 1969) has described the predictable stages of dying. In so doing she has described the stages of loss and grief itself.

Explain to learners that losing anyone or anything is like a small death. Our response is similar whether to actual death or to symbolic deaths. Grief is the reaction to whatever the mind interprets as loss.

Write the names of the stages and key words on the board as you explain the stages as masterfully defined by Dr. Kubler-Ross.

a. **Stage 1: Denial and Isolation**

"*Oh, no, it can't be!*" we lament. We deny that the loss has happened. Denial takes many forms including, "*I don't care.*" The "*I don't care*" that follows loss means, "*It hurts too much to care.*" It is a **denial of pain,** not genuine apathy. The retreat into isolation is an attempt to escape in order to avoid pain.

That retreat also is due to the press of **healthy ego** that drives us through the process of loss and detachment to discover our inner strength. The experience of **detachment** is necessary to shape valid individuality. For most people detachment is imposed by external events that produce loss.

b. **Stage 2: Anger**

As we have seen, when ego has identified some object with self, having it taken away is most threatening. The experience may be as threatening as any attack on self.

Since anger is the natural and normal **reaction to threat,** anger at the loss is inevitable. This is true whether or not the loss was in any way voluntary. When loss is sudden and imposed from without, the anger of grief is often rageful.

c. **Stage 3: Bargaining**

Dr. Kubler-Ross described this stage as some sort of **agreement with God** to postpone the inevitable. It consists of a promise of some type of good behavior in exchange for some favor. The favor may be more time or time to witness some special event such as a child's wedding or graduation. It usually includes a deadline (the wedding or graduation) and a promise that the person will not ask for more if the wish is granted. The wish is usually kept secret.

The emotion here is **guilt,** asking for one more chance to make up for past missed opportunities. Although this stage more clearly applies to the infirm who know they are dying, we may find parallels in other types of loss. For example, the alcoholic promises to stop drinking in exchange for reconciliation with a spouse. The girlfriend or boyfriend promises to attend to the absent loved one's every need if only the couple reunite. The small child promises God, "*I'll be good,*" if the lost, cherished toy is found. Ball teams promise amazing things for victory.

We bargain, promise, and haggle, so great is our fear of loss.

d. **Stage 4: Depression (Sadness)**

Sooner or later the bargaining stops and the anger fades. We are left then with the heart of grief, **profound sadness.** Sorrow, weeping, and feelings of emptiness and purposelessness predominate. Appropriate and **openly experienced** expression of these feelings is known as **mourning.**

But inappropriate, excessive, and prolonged sadness is called **depression.** Mourning is an acceptable and necessary part of the human condition. Depression is not. As America's number one mental illness, the phenomenon of depression requires a lesson of its own in our study, Lesson Eighteen.

e. **Stage 5: Acceptance**

The final stage, acceptance, follows mourning. Acceptance is the **release** of anger, guilt, and the other strong emotions that maintained the attachment. Acceptance is not just a mental recognition that what is lost is irretrievable. Acceptance is an actual **emotional** and **cognitive shift.**

Usually, making the shift requires a cognitive reinterpretation of the loss, such as, *"Yes, he's dead, but that does not mean I'll never see him again. I'll see him in heaven."* Or, *"Yes, the relationship is over, but that does not mean my life is over. I'll love again."*

We often **refuse to let go** because it feels as if letting go of the strong emotions is the final letting go of the person or lost object. Refusal to let go results when we have **overidentified** with the object of loss. Letting go is internally experienced as the release of such an essential part of oneself that the choice is seen as impossible.

True release lets go of the attachment and the identification *or* reinterprets that identification on another level. For example, such a reinterpretation is shown in the shifting of self-talk from, *"I can't live without this person,"* to *"God must have a reason for this. I may not understand, but I will go on."* Then release is followed by quiet emptiness, the serenity of peace, and the hope that the emptiness and peace will create the space for new attachments, new identifications.

ACTIVITIES

Choose one or a combination. Assign one for carryover.

1. **Journaling—"A Letter to Me"**

An exploration of the epidemic of teen suicide today reveals the sad fact that breaking up with a boyfriend or girlfriend may precipitate suicide, self-destructive behavior, or suicidal ideation. "Puppy love" is no longer taken in stride as part of the inevitable ups and downs of adolescence. Society's failure to teach the young how to grieve is highlighted when teens overreact to loss with violent, self-destructive and other hostile behavior.

Direct learners to write a letter to themselves in their journals about a relationship that produced loss and grief. Learners are to pretend they are their own "best friend" writing to give consolation and advice on how to handle the loss. Direct them to use what they now know about loss and attachment as they explore the meaning of the relationship in their lives.

Common losses they may write about include: the loss of a pet, the loss of friends after moving to another school, the loss of a close friend after an argument, the loss of a girlfriend or boyfriend, the loss of a parent's presence in the home due to divorce, and the loss of a grandparent who died.

2. **A Poem on Grief**

Direct learners to write a poem of five stanzas on the five stages of grief. Each stanza is to describe one of the five stages. Encourage learners who have experienced a personal loss of a close relative by death or divorce to use that experience as the theme of the poem. Other learners may use a lesser personal loss or another topic such as the death of a popular movie star or public figure.

3. **"List of Feeling Words" Activity**
   (Activity Sheet 17.1)

Distribute the list of synonyms for grief, guilt, shame, and other uncomfortable emotions. Direct learners to use the first column on grief to relate the story of "A Disappointment." Stories may be oral or written.

BULLETIN BOARD MATERIAL

1. Without a hurt, the heart is hollow.

2. *Man is not disturbed by events, but by the view he takes of them.*

Epictetus

Name: _____   Date: _____

Activity Sheet 17.1
LIST OF FEELING WORDS

GRIEF

Mild Grief	Moderate Grief	Intense Grief
disappointed	dejected	disillusioned
pathetic	sad	pitiful
dismal	melancholic	sorrowful
gloomy	unhappy	cheerless
discouraged	disheartened	dispirited
downcast	heartsick	crestfallen
morose	woeful	desolate
blue	glum	dolorous
somber	mournful	pining
downhearted	despondent	disconsolate
grieving	lamenting	languishing
discontented	miserable	heartbroken
displeased	dissatisfied	disgruntled

GUILT and SHAME		**OTHER CHALLENGING EMOTIONS**	
Mild	**Strong**	**Mild**	**Strong**
culpable	guilty	possessive	jealous
sorrowful	contrite	covetous	envious
apologetic	repentant	suspicious	paranoid
sorry	penitent	smug	haughty
regretful	remorseful	proud	arrogant
ashamed	abashed	conceited	vain
chagrined	embarrassed	indifferent	apathetic
humiliated	mortified	detached	impervious
belittled	shamed	unconcerned	nonchalant
		sickening	revolting
		offended	repelled
		disgusted	nauseated

*Permission granted to reproduce for classroom use. Taken from **Affective Self-Esteem** by Katherine Krefft, M.Ed., Ph.D. © 1993, Accelerated Development Inc., Publishers, 3808 W. Kilgore Avenue, Muncie, IN 47304-4896.*

EIGHTEEN

THE DARK SORCERER

OBJECTIVES

Learners will demonstrate their comprehension of

1. the symptoms and types of depression and the factors that encourage depression as manifested by participation in class discussion and a self-analysis;

2. the meaning of suicidal self-talk and what to do when one experiences such self-talk as illustrated by a role-play; and

3. the roles of repression and internalization of anger in the dynamics of depression as shown by writing a summary of the presentation on the "sorcerer's" lies and tricks.

MATERIALS

- Magic Wand

- Chalkboard or overhead projector

- Crayons, slips of paper and brown paper bags

- Journals for learners

- Activity Sheets 5.1, 12.1, and 17.1, the three lists of feeling words, and Activity Sheet 18.1, "Definitions of Composite Emotions"

CONTENT

1. **Review**

   Collect carryover assignment. Review the last lesson.

   - What is grief?

   - What process must happen before grief can be felt?

- Name three types of loss.

- Compare and contrast valid versus invalid grief.

- What is emotional enmeshment?

- What is healthy, mature attachment?

- What emotion is behind jealousy?

- Describe how invalid expectations produce invalid grief.

- List the two steps that must precede mature love.

- Name the physician and book that describes the stages of dying, loss, and grief.

- List and describe the four stages of loss and grief.

- After a profound hurt, what does *"I don't care"* mean?

- Explain why and how anger is a part of grieving.

- What is mourning? (Spell or write out the word.)

- What is acceptance?

- Why do we often refuse to let go of the strong emotions of mourning?

- How have you used what you have learned?

2. **The Sorcerer Thief**

   Instruct learners, *"If emotions are like magic, then depression is like an evil sorcerer. This dark sorcerer transforms light into darkness, freedom into imprisonment, and joy into sorrow. The sorcerer seems to have great power. The power of that darkness creates more darkness until at last it seems there is no hope.*

   "But that great power is an illusion, a trick. It is a very sly trick, but it is a trick. It is a trick because the dark sorcerer steals all that power from YOU. The way to defeat the sorcerer is to take the power back. The way to win the battle of depression is not to let yourself be fooled. YOU have the power to banish the dark sorcerer from your life. In this lesson we're going to learn how."

3. **Symptoms of Depression**

   Explain to learners that the difference between mourning and depression is vast. Openly **mourning** a valid loss is acceptable. **Brooding** endlessly in depression is not. Depression is not a fated or inevitable condition. Even when a marked physiological component is present, the individual still has choices that can be made.

Severe, prolonged depression is characterized by *several* of these symptoms:

- feelings of worthlessness and hopelessness;
- prolonged, frequent, and uncontrollable crying;
- numb feelings or apparent inability to feel;
- withdrawal and isolation;
- misuse of alcohol and drugs;
- appetite changes: extreme weight loss or gain;
- sleep disturbances: insomnia or hypersomnia;
- chronic fatigue or low energy;
- irritability: over and/or underreacting;
- poor attention and indecisiveness; and/or
- suicidal self-talk.

Write the following heading on the board.

SYMPTOMS OF DEPRESSION

Then, pass the wand to elicit learners' input as you list the symptoms. Begin by asking, *"How do **you** feel when you are depressed? What do you **do** that shows you are depressed? What is your self-talk when you are depressed?"*

4. **The Dumbest Choice**

Explain to learners, *"Having thoughts of suicide does not mean you **really** want to kill yourself. Actually, many, perhaps most, people have thoughts of suicide at one time or other in their life. Suicidal self-talk means that you feel completely overwhelmed and want to escape.*

*"Suicidal self-talk means the emotions of fear, anger, and guilt are interfering with your ability to think logically. In the confusion you **temporarily** cannot figure out a sensible way to meet the challenge. Suicidal self-talk is determined by feelings, not reason."*

Continue the explanation by describing the warning bell.

a. **A Warning Bell**

*"Suicidal self-talk is like a bell going off in your head. The bell says, 'It's getting too hot for me to handle. Go get help. Go get help **now.**' Suicidal self-talk does not mean you're crazy; it means you need help.*

"Suicidal self-talk also may be likened to a smoke alarm going off. What is the proper thing to do if a smoke alarm goes off?" Accept various answers. It may be a false alarm. However, the reasonable thing to do is to check it out and see if there is a source of smoke. If the source of the smoke is extinguished at an early stage, the house need not burn down. The same is true with suicidal self-talk.

b. **Putting Out The Fire**

"The thing to do is to hear that self-talk as the warning it is. Now, if your house were burning down, you would not expect to put the fire out with a garden hose. No, you would call the professionals. You would call the fire department. It's the same with suicidal self-talk.

*"If the thoughts are frequent and persistent, it's like a fire in your house. If you can't put it out by yourself, go get help. That is what you are **supposed** to do. That is the okay thing to do.*

"So, the thing to do is to talk to your parents or pastor or a counselor until you come up with another, acceptable way out of the difficulty. Find someone with whom you can talk. Then, keep talking until you get the situation settled and the suicidal self-talk goes away.

"Suicide is not smart. Suicide is dumb. Suicide is never okay. Suicide is like throwing the baby out with the bath water. Suicide is like getting a spot on your shirt and then jumping with your whole body into the washing machine. Sure, that will get the spot off your shirt, but really!

"Reasonable people who have learned how to constructively handle emotions can find other solutions. It's often said that suicide is a permanent solution to a temporary problem. As such, it is the dumbest choice anyone may make."

5. **Types of Depression**

Indicate the other symptoms of depression you have listed on the board. *"Now, let's go back to these other symptoms of depression. Most depression does not get so bad that we get to the point of suicidal self-talk."*

Explain to learners that depression has two types. **Preparatory depression** is caused by anticipation of an expected loss. When we know a loss is coming, we may mourn it ahead of time. We also may be depressed about it in advance. The second type of depression, **reactive depression,** comes after the event has happened.

Most depression is of the second type. Depression is caused by the repression of uncomfortable emotions. **Repression** is a psychological defense in which the mind conveniently forgets uncomfortable emotions in order to push them away. The process of repression is unconscious; that is, we do it yet do not realize we are doing it. On the other hand **suppression** is a conscious process. We are aware of the avoidant behavior. In mourning we do not repress the emotions.

a. **The Sorcerer's Lies**

Direct learners to pay close attention and take notes since at the conclusion of the following segments they will write in their own words what you have said.

Begin with, *"Now we'll see how the sorcerer uses tricks and lies to get us depressed. Repression is the dark sorcerer's main trick. Repression says, 'If I just don't think about this, I'll be okay. If I pretend it isn't there, it'll go away.' The sorcerer would have us believe everything is okay when our hearts know this is not true.*

"The sorcerer says, 'You're not really angry, a good little [boy or girl] like you! Besides, you have nothing to be guilty or ashamed about. It was all the fault of those other people, you know that. You're not sad! Have a drink! You deserve to feel only good feelings.'

*"With lies like this, the sorcerer pulls us away from our true feelings of fear, anger, guilt, shame, and sadness. These feelings are neither good nor bad. We feel what we feel. We have a **right** to feel what we feel. Experiencing uncomfortable emotions is part of being human, pure and simple.*

*"The way to beat the dark sorcerer is to reclaim our true feelings, **no matter how painful.** 'You can't fool me, dark sorcerer! I'm mad and I know I am. And I wish I didn't, but I feel guilty, too. I feel lonely and scared and, right or wrong, that's the way I feel!'*

"The way to win is to take our real emotions back and not let anyone or anything tell us we are not feeling what our hearts know we are feeling. We can let the dark sorcerer cast us into the black pit of depression. Or we can cast the sorcerer into the pit by proudly and fiercely owning, feeling, and positively expressing our emotions."

b. **The Sorcerer's Anger Trick**

Of all the uncomfortable emotions used by the dark sorcerer anger stands out foremost. Depression may be the effect of repressed fear, guilt, and sadness. But in suicidal and other intense depression anger is the key emotion. In a trick more amazing than any slight of hand the sorcerer turns anger, a force intended to motivate us to self-protection and constructive defense, destructively against us.

Explain to learners that all hostile, destructive acts are acts of anger—no matter how "cool" one feels while engaged in them. This is why

DEPRESSION IS ANGER TURNED INWARD.

Write the statement on the board as you emphasize that **suicide, too, is an act of anger.** Suicide is the ultimate act of anger turned inward. Acts of hostility are acts of anger whether or not the perpetrator "feels" angry while engaging in the hostility. Thus, a nation's assault, rape, suicide, and murder rates combined could be termed its anger index.

Stop here and allow learners to write in their own words an explanation of the sorcerer's lies and tricks. Share or collect their written paragraphs for later feedback.

6. The Sorcerer's Accomplices

Explain to learners though repressed emotions are the root cause of most depression, many other factors also lead to and encourage depression. As you pass the wand, lead learners in a discussion as you write each item on the board. Invite them to look for the item or items that apply more particularly to them.

7. Factors That Encourage Depression

- Fear of and denial of emotions. Refusal to feel what we know we are indeed feeling, what any normal human being would feel in similar circumstances.

- False beliefs.

    "Be strong." (A highly deceptive injunction that really means, *"Don't feel. Don't have or express emotions."*)

    "Don't cry."

    "I can't live without you."

    "I can't take it."

    "Things are never going to change."

    "Missing someone is a sign you love them." (Missing someone is a sign you are attached to them. It may or may not mean you love them.)

- Ignorance about what feelings are normal and natural.

- Refusal to accept pain as part of the human condition.

- Drugs and alcohol. Alcohol is a short-term stimulant but soon after, a depressant. Drugs interfere with the natural biochemical cycles of emotion.

- Physiological effects of disturbances in the sleep cycle. Most Americans do not get enough sleep.

- Other physiological changes in body chemistry. Severe, intractable depression may require medical intervention.

- Elimination of rituals for mourning in society as a whole. Black clothing, arm bands, wreaths on the door, and anniversary religious rituals belong to times past.

ACTIVITIES

Choose one or a combination. Assign one for carryover.

1. **"Lists of Feeling Words" Activity**
   (Activity Sheets 5.1, 12.1, and 17.1)

   Learners are now able to complete a self-analysis of depression. Direct them to use *all three* lists of feeling words along with what they have learned in this lesson to write an essay, "My Own Depression." In the essay learners describe their own: (1) self-talk, (2) emotions, and (3) behavior when they are depressed.

   Writing the following questions on the board may prove helpful.

   When you are depressed

   - **What is your self-talk?**
   - **How do you feel physically?**
   - **What are your emotions?**
   - **What do you do? How do you act?**
   - **How do you use alcohol and drugs?**
   - **How do you get yourself out of depression?**

   ---

2. **Role-Play**

   Divide the class into groups consisting of three members each. Instruct learners, *"Each group is to invent a scenario in which one learner plays the role of someone who is experiencing suicidal self-talk. The other two may play whichever roles their group chooses. Their goal is to help the suicidal person through the crisis. You'll make up your roles and then take turns acting them out."*

   Although learners should have latitude for creativity, the teacher should circulate and give enough guidance so that at least some of the groups choose to make one of the two supportive roles that of a teacher, counselor, pastor, psychologist, or other professional. Undoubtedly, one of the supportive roles will be that of a friend. But when suicidal self-talk is severe, friends may best help their friends by guiding them to a professional helper.

3. **Sad Sacks Activity**
   "List of Feeling Words" (Activity Sheet 17.1)

   Divide learners into groups consisting of two persons each. Distribute crayons, small slips of paper, and one brown paper bag per pair.

Instruct learners, *"Each person is to first talk for three minutes [or longer] about what makes you sad. Use the Grief List, Activity Sheet 17.1, as a guide to express your feelings. As the person talks, write on the strips of paper what they say makes them sad. Put **one** sad thing and **one** word from the Grief List on each separate slip of paper.*

"After six minutes, both of you together are to draw and color a face on the bag. That's your 'Sad Sack' face so make it sad enough to fit all the words the two of you chose from the list. Inside the bag put the paper slips.

"We'll stop when I tell you. Then, you'll get up by twos and alternate to pull the slips from the bag and talk about your Sad Sack's sad feelings."

The above format is designed to develop the social skills of cooperation, teamwork, and empathy. Alternately, each learner may design an individual Sad Sack.

4. **Journaling—Composite Emotions**
   "Definitions of Composite Emotions" (Activity Sheet 18.1)

As society progresses, old usages of words are modified. New words are invented to reflect new understandings. New words also may reflect consensually shared **misunderstandings.** This is especially true of the words used to describe emotions.

"I'm under so much stress" and *"I feel so pressured"* are modern equivalents of *"I'm scared and angry."* What is called "stress" is simply emotion in a modern guise. *"He copped an attitude on me"* is a disguise for *"He's angry at me."* As usually used, "an attitude" is a stance of angry arrogance that combines anger and aloof pride.

Whether one is stressed, pressured, or has an attitude, it is all just emotion. Resolve the emotion and the stress and pressure vanish. Change the self-talk that underlies an attitude and a real human being, probably one that is hurting badly, emerges.

Share Activity Sheet 18.1 with learners. Lead a discussion on the many words that are disguises for and elaborations of our simple, raw emotions of fear, anger, grief, and guilt. Then, have learners write in their journals which of the composite emotions apply most personally to them and why.

Note to the Teacher

All professionals should be aware of symptoms of serious depression and emotional disturbance that may require professional intervention. Some of these are prolonged withdrawal and silence, preoccupation with themes of death and destruction, refusal to eat, lack of care for hygiene and personal appearance, night terrors, apparent inability to feel pain, self-mutilation, fire setting, grossly inappropriate social behavior, drug use and other escapist behavior. These may signify depression or other serious emotional illness.

BULLETIN BOARD MATERIAL

1. *No one really knows enough to be a pessimist.*
   Norman Cousins

Name: _____ Date: _____

Activity Sheet 18.1
DEFINITIONS OF COMPOSITE EMOTIONS

Upset: Often anger. Frequently fear and grief as well.
  "I feel upset" = "I feel emotion, but I don't want to tell myself what precisely it is I'm feeling."

Depressed: Anger turned inward. Grief. Fear and guilt. Severe depression: grief and guilt mixed with anger and fear.
  "It's too depressing" = "I am depressed."

Confused: Presence of more than one emotion at one time. Ask yourself, *"What am I afraid about? Angry about? Sad about? Guilty about?"*

Bad: Bad is not a feeling. *"I feel bad"* is used to indicate many emotions: guilt, sadness, fear, anger as well as to refer to physical illness and fatigue.

Hurt: Anger, resentment, and grief turned inward. Some fear also may be present.

Distressed: Anxiety or embarrassment or grief or irritation in combination. Also, a rough synonym for upset.

Sullen: Anger plus sadness.

Frustrated: Anger plus the belief that one is unable to act.

Lonely: Fear, hurt, and sadness experienced in isolation. Frequently, grief and anger, too.

Dismay: Anxiety, fear, and disappointment.

Self-pity: Wallowing in anger over disappointment, guilt, and sadness.

Moody: Tendency to demonstrate emotions and to allow them to determine external behavior. Moody usually combines sadness with another emotion.

Pressured: A modern usage meaning fear and urgency.
  "I'm under so much pressure" = "I'm afraid I cannot meet what I perceive as urgent demands."

Stressed: Usually, anger primarily and fear secondarily. May also indicate grief and guilt. "Stressed out" is a modern synonym for upset. Neither usage gives any information on the truth of what one is really feeling.

Attitude: Angry arrogance. Anger combined with aloof pride. A protective position to hide fear and hurt.

*Permission granted to reproduce for classroom use. Taken from **Affective Self-Esteem** by Katherine Krefft, M.Ed., Ph.D. © 1993, Accelerated Development Inc., Publishers, 3808 W. Kilgore Avenue, Muncie, IN 47304-4896.*

GOOD GRIEF

OBJECTIVES

Learners will demonstrate their comprehension of

1. the process of healing from grief and depression and the value of loss as demonstrated by participation in class discussion and written exercises;

2. constructive versus destructive identification and the two paths of grief as manifested by composing stories about two people who took different paths; and

3. a wise man's three-step prescription for healing from grief as evidenced by applying those steps and other information from this lesson to help a grieving friend.

MATERIALS

• Magic Wand

• Chalkboard or overhead projector

• Journals for learners

• Activity Sheets 17.1, "List of Feeling Words," and 19.1, "Happy Emotions"

CONTENT

1. **Review**

   Collect carryover assignment. Review the last lesson.

   • Why do we call depression the dark sorcerer?

   • From where does the power of the dark sorcerer come?

   • How can you destroy the power of the dark sorcerer?

- What is the difference between mourning and depression?

- List the symptoms of depression.

- What is the true meaning of suicidal self-talk?

- What is the thing to do if you have difficulty getting rid of suicidal self-talk?

- Is suicide okay? Why or why not?

- Name one reason suicide is dumb.

- Name and describe two types of depression.

- What is the root cause of most depression?

- Explain how repression works. Why do we use it?

- Why is repression the sorcerer's main trick?

- How can we undo the sorcerer's work?

- Of all the emotions which is key in depression?

- Explain the meaning of, *"Depression is anger turned inward,"* and *"Suicide is an act of anger."*

- List several factors that lead to depression.

- How have you used what you have learned?

- Close your eyes. What is on the bulletin board?

2. **Healing from Grief and Depression**

Remind learners that in the last two lessons we have looked at the causes of depression and the difference between mourning and depression. In mourning we openly express and allow ourselves to feel the uncomfortable feelings. But in depression we repress the emotions, that is, we shove them underground.

The words allow for a little word play. In ***mourning*** we usually feel a little better in the ***morning.*** But when we ***re***press, we get ***de***pressed. In mourning we still have the ability to say, *"Tomorrow is another day."* In depression the sorcerer whispers, *"There is no tomorrow."*

a. **The Value of Loss**

Explain that both mourning and depression provide us with opportunities to develop our inner resources. Loss may lead us to discover ***inner strength.*** From loss comes ***detachment.***

Detached and alone, we must seek individuality and independence. Diagram the process on the board.

> **Loss → Detachment → Independence**

Several valuable qualities seem to require the experience of profound grief. Grief is Good Grief because it creates empathy, compassion, and constructive social and personal action. Add the following to the board.

> **GOOD GRIEF PRODUCES**
>
> 1. **Constructive action**
> 2. **Empathy and compassion**

Explain to learners that grief may motivate us to live for the best qualities which the lost loved one represented. A natural healing process whereby we incorporate the loss into the self is called *identification.* That identification makes us one with our loss and thus negates it. We make what we have lost a part of ourselves to magically undo the loss.

For example, George Burns reports he slept in his wife, Gracie's, bed after she died. Bob Kennedy wore his brother's jacket after the President died. Eleanor Roosevelt devoted herself to the social and political issues that had concerned her husband. Similarly, Coretta Scott King has devoted herself to human rights. More common examples also are evident as when a young girl wears her brother's sunglasses right after his funeral.

b. **Constructive versus Destructive Identification**

But the identification that proceeds from grief may be destructive as well as constructive. It is **constructive** when it results in constructive activities that are in line with the valid desires of self. Identification is **destructive** when it results in destructive activities and is NOT congruent with who one really is. Forcing oneself to live forever in the shadow of a dead loved one is unhealthy. For example, Queen Victoria mourned for decades after her husband, Albert's, death.

The most serious consequence of such misplaced loyalty is **survivor guilt.** In fact, the inability to separate one's identity from that of the dead loved one may result in one's own death. Frequently, a spouse dies a few years after the death of a beloved husband or wife.

One determines whether identification is positive or negative by the activities it produces and by the measure of happiness brought or denied. If one is happy and content with a constructive life brought about by the identification, then grief is transformed into Good Grief.

Another facet of Good Grief is the empathy, love, and compassion it produces. Since the experience of loss is universal, grief may induce profound empathy for our common humanity. Grief takes the air out of the most inflated egos. No one can prevent all loss from touching their lives. No one is above or below the experience of death.

Other experiences may produce empathy, but grief must be actively channeled into Good Grief to do so. The alternative may be bitterness and emptiness. Diagram the following on the board.

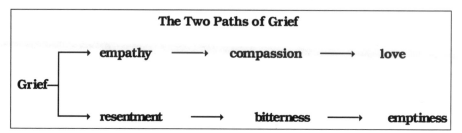

Explain to learners that **empathy** is mostly feeling, not thinking. Empathy is **emotional sensitivity** to another's feelings. Empathy is feeling *with* the other. **Sympathy** is mental commiseration for the other, feeling *for* them, pity. Empathy is 80% emotion and 20% thinking. Sympathy is the reverse.

Genuine empathy produces **compassion.** Compassion is the active part of empathy. Empathy is feeling. Compassion is acting. Compassion is shown in acts of good-will, charity, and mercy. Compassion is the feeling, the empathy, *with* the expression.

Actively expressing altruistic benevolence is called **love.** Love is unselfish good-will and clemency actively expressed. The **highest form of love** is a decision, a mental act, not a feeling. In this sense we may love those we do not like. Love may exist without warm, cozy feeling.

Love is also the **decision to forgive.** Often deep depression does not lift until the person decides to forgive and release the past. In grief forgiving the dead person for dying is sometimes necessary.

As we have seen, to say, *"I forgive but I won't forget,"* means *"Mentally, I am forgiving because I have been taught that's the right thing to do. But I'm hanging onto the emotions."* The rage and bitterness one feels over the loss are kept, not released.

"I can't forget that event" means *"I have not yet been able to relieve myself of the emotions occasioned by that event."* Open and honest expression of emotions as taught in these lessons is the path to forgetting as well as to forgiving in all types of loss.

We have learned that grief is sorrow, a valid human emotion. When experienced, grief does lessen with time. Depression may not. Grief like all emotions comes in waves. One may learn to go with the flow. But depression is like a flood surge that ever remains at high tide. Grief ebbs and recedes.

Depression suffocates. We may learn to convert grief into empathy and compassion. It is very difficult to find a positive purpose for depression.

4. The George Burns' Prescription

As we saw in Lesson Fourteen, crying is Nature's healing washing machine. No one has better expressed nature's prescription for grief than George Burns, the irrepressible comedian. He was speaking of his own grief for his beloved wife, Gracie, when at age 93 he said, *"What do you do when someone dies? You cry and you keep crying until you stop crying."*[6] Write the following on the board.

```
Burn's Prescription for Grief

1. You cry.
2. You keep crying.
3. You stop crying.
```

Explain to learners the importance of allowing Burn's three steps to occur. Taking an "I'll cry tomorrow" attitude is a form of denial. Continue, *"As you grieve, allow for each stage of grief, including anger. The emotion may take the form of anger at God, at the departed, at survivors, at oneself. Allow the sadness by crying and moods of melancholy.*

*"Be aware that periods of emotional pain may alternate with the opposite, **emotional numbness,** periods when you seem to be able to feel little or nothing. Finally, show your acceptance by taking active steps to adjust to life."*

Remind learners that as with all emotional expression, remembering the A, B, C's is the key to the constructive handling of grief. Write these steps on the board.

```
A. Allow the grief.
   Recognize and admit your feelings.

B. Be with the grief.
   Feel the sadness and other emotions.

C. Channel the grief.
   Take constructive action.
```

6 Burns, G. (1980). The statement was made on a television talk show. See also his 1980 autobiography, *The third time around.* New York: Putnam.

ACTIVITIES

Choose one or a combination. Assign one for carryover.

1. **Journaling—A Letter to Your Son or Daughter**

   Direct learners to write a letter in their journals. Instruct them, *"Pretend it is many, many years from now. You have a wonderful spouse and children. You have lived many fruitful, happy years. Write a letter to be delivered to your son, daughter, or children after your death. Write words to help them heal from their grief and to understand the value of loss. You may make it a letter written before you died or a letter from heaven, as you prefer."*

2. **The Two Brothers or Sisters**

   Remind learners of the two paths of grief—destructive as well as constructive identification. Direct them to tell the tale of "The Two Brothers" or "The Two Sisters" in which one sibling takes one path and the other takes the opposite path.

   Stories may be written or oral. If oral, let learners one by one add a sentence to the story. The teacher may begin, *"Once there were two people in the same family who took very opposite paths after a loved one died."*

3. **A Letter to a Friend or Relative**

   Direct learners to write a letter to a friend or relative who is grieving. Instruct them to include in the body of the letter Burns' Prescription and whatever else they have learned that may be of help to the bereaved.

   Learners whose families have experienced recent, actual losses may write real letters which may be mailed with the teacher's approval. Other learners may invent a loss and write what they imagine they would say.

4. **"List of Feeling Words" Activity**
   (Activity Sheet 17.1)

   Invite learners to compose a poem or essay entitled, "Desolation," about the time they felt most desolate. Direct them to use words from the third column of Activity Sheet 17.1.

5. **"Happy Emotions"**
   (Activity Sheet 19.1)

   The "Happy Emotions" activity sheets may be used in parallel fashion to the other lists of feelings. See previous activities.

BULLETIN BOARD MATERIAL

1. God mends the broken hearts that yield up all the pieces.

2. *Forgiveness is a gift you give yourself.*
   Oprah Winfrey

Name: _____ Date: _____

Activity Sheet 19.1
HAPPY EMOTIONS

Mild	Moderate	Intense
cheerful	sunny	excited
courageous	brave	bold
animated	spirited	vivacious
happy	merry	bright
festive	joyous	ecstatic
curious	fascinated	engrossed
hardy	strong	robust
tender	affectionate	devoted
touching	poignant	stirring
exultant	overjoyed	euphoric
safe	secure	self-possessed
content	blithe	happy go lucky
grateful	appreciative	obliged
intent	avid	keen
assured	soothed	tranquil
interested	concerned	intrigued
intent	determined	resolute
proud	magnificent	glorious
longing	sentimental	nostalgic
jolly	mirthful	jovial
glad	contented	complacent
hopeful	encouraged	eager
calm	composed	serene
silly	giddy	ridiculous
splendid	wonderful	fantastic
playful	frisky	jaunty
free	independent	self-reliant
fine	splendid	sublime
romantic	amorous	passionate

*Permission granted to reproduce for classroom use. Taken from **Affective Self-Esteem** by Katherine Krefft, M.Ed., Ph.D.
© 1993, Accelerated Development Inc., Publishers, 3808 W. Kilgore Avenue, Muncie, IN 47304-4896.*

Name: _____   Date: _____

Activity Sheet 19.1 (Continued)

Mild	Moderate	Intense
fanciful	flighty	frivolous
quiet	peaceful	placid
pleasant	comfortable	cozy
reassured	comforted	forgiving
earnest	fervent	vehement
warm	cheery	lighthearted
excited	electrified	delirious
motivated	heartened	inspired
firm	steady	unwavering
emotional	mushy	maudlin
delighted	enthralled	blissful
merry	buoyant	jovial
elated	exuberant	jubilant
aghast	astonished	stunned
friendly	genial	affable
pleased	satisfied	fulfilled
close	affectionate	loving
kind	tender	compassionate
sensual	sexy	erotic
playful	whimsical	capricious
joyful	elated	delighted
trusting	confident	certain
ardent	enthusiastic	zealous
lively	energetic	high spirited
raving	effervescing	gushing
invigorated	exhilarated	rejuvenated
thrilled	enchanted	rapturous
startled	surprised	shocked

*Permission granted to reproduce for classroom use. Taken from **Affective Self-Esteem** by Katherine Krefft, M.Ed., Ph.D.*
© 1993, Accelerated Development Inc., Publishers, 3808 W. Kilgore Avenue, Muncie, IN 47304-4896.

UNIT V:
GUILT

THE ICKY, YUCKY BLOB

OBJECTIVES

NOTES

Learners will demonstrate their comprehension of

1. the nature of guilt as a reaction to failed expectations as demonstrated by participating in class discussion, finishing incomplete sentences, and by self-analysis;

2. the differences between valid guilt and invalid guilt as shown by participation in class discussion; and

3. the central role of should self-talk in guilt and how to constructively channel guilt as illustrated by working with a personal Should List and by self-analysis.

MATERIALS

• Magic Wand

• Chalkboard or overhead projector

• Journals for learners

• Activity Sheets 17.1, "List of Feeling Words," and 20.1 and 20.2, "Decisions, Not Emotions"

CONTENT

1. **Review**

Collect carryover assignment. Review the last lesson.

• What play on words helps us remember the difference between mourning and depression?

• How is loss related to independence?

• What is Good Grief? What does it produce?

- What is the psychological process of identification?

- Give an example of identification after loss.

- What is survivor guilt?

- How do we tell if identification is positive?

- Diagram the two paths of grief.

- Describe the differences and similarities between these pairs of concepts: empathy and sympathy, empathy and compassion, sympathy and compassion, empathy and love, compassion and love.

- How is refusal to forgive related to depression?

- A friend says, *"I forgive but I can't forget."* What do you say to console and help?

- List the steps in Burns' Prescription for grieving.

- What is emotional numbness? When might it happen?

- If you were grieving and found you were mad at God, what would you do?

- Apply the A, B, C's to grief.

- How have you used what you have learned?

2. **The Sorcerer's Cousin**

Explain to learners, *"Guilt is like an icky, yucky blob that covers the skin. It sticks fast, feels terrible, and is hard to remove. Guilt is difficult to handle because removing it may feel like your skin is being peeled off, slowly. Guilt is a second skin that like cancer does not know when to stop growing.*

"The yuck blob and the dark sorcerer are first cousins. Both are con artists, tricksters. Both fool us into believing the worst. Both are liars and thieves. They steal their power from us. Not only do they lie to us. They make us lie about ourselves! Guilt added to depression yields a case of the Major Miseries."

Diagram the following on the board.

> **Guilt + Depression = The Major Miseries**

Then continue, *"The emotions present in the Major Miseries are so painful that often people attempt to allay them by resorting to drinking and drug use. That just worsens the cycle because upon sobering up the person feels even more guilty and more depressed. Yuck blob guilt and valid guilt are so different that they really do not deserve the same word, guilt, to name them."*

3. **Guilt: The Most Human Emotion**

Explain, *"Guilt is a particularly human emotion. When we observe animal behavior, it appears that most animals experience fear. It also appears that many animal species experience anger. It seems that some even demonstrate grief. But guilt?"*

As you lead learners in a discussion of the emotions animals show, ask, *"Do you think animals ever feel guilty?"* Some learner may point out the behavior of naughty dogs and cats, behavior that appears "guilty." But is it guilt or fear of punishment? Dolphins and dogs exhibit loyalty, but do they do it out of guilt?

Continue, *"Guilt is uniquely human. Guilt is the invention of the human race.* **Guilt is felt** *when one does not live up to the* **expectations** *of the one's* **moral code.** *We know our expectations by our self-talk, 'I* **should** *do this, I should not do that.'*

"Animals may exhibit fine traits: loyalty, devotion, perseverance. But it is doubtful that animals have a moral code in the human sense. Dogs and cats do not say 'should.'"

Diagram and leave the following on the board.

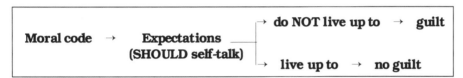

Finally, sum up by sharing with learners that the validity of one's guilt, then, stems ultimately from the validity of one's moral code. Defining an appropriate moral code is beyond the scope of these lessons. Examining collective beliefs about shoulds and should nots is.

a. **Valid vs. Invalid Guilt**

Valid guilt derives from the recognition that one has failed to live up to one's own, freely chosen code. Valid guilt, by definition, cannot be imposed from outside.

Valid guilt is keen disappointment in oneself for not being true to a code one has chosen and believes in. Valid guilt is healthy guilt. It is a plausible drop in self-esteem due to a mistake, an error in judgment, a temporary failing, even though a serious mistake.

Healthy guilt is the mother of **humility.** No one is perfect. No one lives up to their moral code 100% of the time. Valid, healthy guilt spurs us to resolve to do better in the future. Healthy guilt is temporary and far from paralyzing. Valid guilt is the response of a healthy ego that does not come undone by disappointment in self.

But of all the qualities that mark healthy guilt and distinguish it from the yuck blob the most singular is *self-forgiveness.* In healthy guilt we forgive ourselves and move on. In unhealthy, invalid guilt we do not.

Unhealthy guilt, the yuck blob, feeds on secret pride. We can't believe we did what we did. How could our actions have been so "bad"? Our pride, our self-esteem, is crushed.

The very act of forgiving ourselves is felt as an admission that we are less than we would like to believe. When self-esteem is uniquely tied to the belief one is a "good" person, then recognition of "bad" behavior is a devastating blow to ego. The yuck blob paralyzes us with such disappointment.

Pass the wand to elicit learners' input as you compare and contrast valid and invalid guilt. Place learners' contributions on the board in a chart similar to the following.

	Valid Guilt	**The Yuck Blob**
Moral Code	Freely Chosen	Imposed by society
Expectations	Reasonable	Unreasonable
SHOULD means	Is constructive Is profitable Is helpful	An unconditional, absolute MUST
Disappointment	In a mistake	In a terrible moral failure
Drop-in Self-esteem	Plausible & Temporary	Paralyzing & Enduring
Ego	Healthy	Unhealthy
Self-forgiveness	Yes	No
Moral Quality	Humility	Pride
Outcome	A better human being	An emotional wreck Drug/alcohol abuse

What becomes clear from this listing is that true, valid guilt has little in common with invalid guilt except for the name. The yuck blob is a tragic **distortion** of healthy guilt even as cancer is a distortion of the normal process of cell growth.

b. **Obsessive-compulsive Disorder**

A strong case of the yuck blob may lead to **Obsessive-compulsive Disorder.** In this emotional illness guilt and anxiety produce three types of symptoms: (1) fear of contamination as shown by behaviors such as repeated hand washing; (2) unreasonable, persistent doubts as shown by behaviors such as checking and rechecking locks and stove top; and, (3) unreasonable guilts such as great guilt over minor matters. Specific fears as well as generalized anxiety also may have a role to play in the disorder.

4. **Defeating the Blob**

The yuck blob may be driven away by following the three basic steps of constructive emotional expression. Write the following on the board.

> **A. Allow the guilt. Admit it.**
>
> **B. Be with the guilt. Feel it.**
>
> **C. Channel the guilt. Take action.**

Explain that in the case of unreasonable guilt the action to be taken usually must include some type of revision of expectations. Sometimes an individual is able to do this alone. But often when expectations are tied into a rigid moral code learned in childhood, talking with parents, teachers, and friends is necessary to sort things out. For some, counseling with a member of the clergy may prove helpful.

Refer back to the diagram placed on the board in number 3, "Guilt: The Most Human Emotion". Point to the central role of expectations in the formation of guilt. Then, add the following to the listing of the A, B, C's already on the board.

> C. **Channel the guilt. Take action.**
> **Explore and change expectations.**
> **Above all, forgive yourself.**

ACTIVITIES

Choose one or a combination. Assign one for carryover.

1. **Incomplete Sentences Activity Using "List of Feeling Words" (Activity Sheet 17.1)**

Direct learners to refer to the columns of Guilt Words on their List of Feeling Words for this exercise. Direct them to write ten sentences that begin *"I feel _____ when . . ."* with the blank filled in with one of the guilt words. Each sentence is to use a different guilt word, e.g., I feel sorry when . . ., I feel ashamed when . . ., I feel humiliated when . . . .

Sentences may be shared in class or in small groups as the teacher judges appropriate.

2. Journaling—Should List

Direct learners, *"At the top of a page in your journal write the title 'Should List.' Write out a list of your should self-talk; for example, 'I should do my homework,' 'People should like me,' and 'No one should hurt another person.' "* If necessary, have learners verbally share items on their lists in order to help others get ideas.

After an appropriate length of time or in a later class, direct learners to number each should. Then, using the same numbers but on a separate page in the notebook, learners write the translation of the should.

Instruct them, *"Now at the top of a new page write the title, 'Translation of Shoulds.' Number by number change the wording of each should statement to make clear what the should is really saying. So, 'I should do my homework' means 'It would be constructive for me to do my homework,' and 'People should like me' becomes 'It would be helpful and nice if people liked me.' What does 'No one should hurt another person' become?"*

Answers will vary. Most shoulds may be translated with variations of "is constructive," "is profitable," "is helpful," and synonyms thereof. Explain that if no constructive translation readily comes to mind, one must then rethink the item. Is it genuinely advantageous? Is it a should one *should* have?

This activity provides an opportunity for learners to explore the use of a thesaurus. Alternately, the following list may be shared on the board or duplicated ahead of time and distributed.

Synonyms for Constructive Shoulding		
Should SHOULD mean		
Is constructive	**Is profitable**	**Is helpful**
effective	fruitful	supportive
practical	gainful	useful
productive	lucrative	beneficial
advantageous	favorable	conducive to
valuable	rewarding	
	worthwhile	

3. How I'll Handle Guilt

Decide before beginning the activity whether or not it will be shared in class. The activity may be done twice, the first time for sharing in class, the second time for sharing only with the teacher or a school counselor. Doing Activity 1 before this one may be helpful.

Instruct learners, *"Think of something you feel guilty about. If there's nothing you now feel guilty about, think about something you have felt guilty about in the past and **pretend** you're still guilty. Apply the elements of Step C, 'Channel the guilt.' Here are some questions that may help you do so."* Conclude as you write the following on the board.

- **What constructive action will you take?**

- **What expectations will you change?**

- **What self-talk will you change?**

- **What new self-talk will you use? List it.**

- **By what actions will you** *show* **you forgive yourself?**

---

4. **"Decisions, Not Emotions"**
   (Activity Sheets 20.1 and 20.2)

   Learners' fund of knowledge about emotions is now at a maximum. They may enjoy discussing and debating Activity Sheets 20.1 and 20.2. The English language allows for a very careless mixing and meshing of **affective** and **cognitive** concepts. Such language usage makes us confuse emotions, the feeling process, with decisions, a mental process.

BULLETIN BOARD MATERIAL

1. Don't SHOULD on yourself.

2. *While forbidden fruit is said to taste sweeter, it usually spoils faster.*

   Abigail Van Buren

Name: _____ Date: _____

Activity Sheet 20.1
DECISIONS, NOT EMOTIONS

Unacceptable Decisions

Despair: The belief that the situation is hopeless coupled with the decision not to try to improve things.

"I'm tired of trying" = "I've allowed my uncomfortable emotions to so overwhelm me that I have little energy to think and act constructively."

Stubbornness: The decision to protect one's ego interests at all costs. The inflation of ego.

Hatred: The decision to project anger outward in actual hostile acts.

"I hate you!" = "I'm furious!"

Revenge: The decision to act on hatred and anger over some wrong or hurt, real or imagined. Aggression.

Prejudice: The decision to project fear outward in anger.

Worthlessness: The decision to believe that one is worth nothing.

"I can't do anything right" = "I have a belief that I can't do anything right, and I feel sad, scared, and angry about it."

Boredom: The decision to believe that other people or external things are responsible for one's entertainment and stimulation. Life is not boring; ask any two-year-old.

"You're boring" = "Don't you know that on this planet you're supposed to entertain me?"

"It's boring" = "My judgment is that this does not interest or stimulate me."

Loneliness: The belief that one is disconnected from people. Lonely is a feeling, but continued loneliness is **choice,** a decision.

Apathy: The decision to hold onto hurt and anger because others, in your judgment, are not interested in you.

"I don't care" = "It hurts too much to care."

"It doesn't matter" = "I have a belief that I don't matter, and since I don't, nothing else does."

Greed: The decision to interpret external things such as money, position, and people as necessary extensions of one's ego, that is, as valued only because they are easy, convenient extensions of one's ego. As an inflation of ego, greed is a denial of and defense against fear.

*Permission granted to reproduce for classroom use. Taken from **Affective Self-Esteem** by Katherine Krefft, M.Ed., Ph.D. © 1993, Accelerated Development Inc., Publishers, 3808 W. Kilgore Avenue, Muncie, IN 47304-4896.*

Name: _____ Date: _____

Activity Sheet 20.2
DECISIONS, NOT EMOTIONS

Constructive Decisions

Understood: The belief that someone else has heard, listened to, and compassionately empathized with one's emotions.

Empathy: The decision to feel with another and to understand his/her emotions. Feeling another's emotions as he/she does. Apathy and noninvolvement are opposites.

Forgiveness: The decision to release hurt and anger.

> *"I forgive you, but I won't forget"* = *"Intellectually, I pardon you,*
> *but I'm hanging onto my hurt and anger."*

The opposite of forgiveness is resentment.

Faith: The decision to trust what cannot be seen or felt. The decision to suspend judgment long enough to allow oneself to experience that which is believed.

For example, to believe in a person is to suspend judgment long enough to allow oneself to experience that person as trustworthy and worthwhile. Faith is given; trust is earned. The opposite of faith is passing judgment.

Hope: The decision to live with expectation and anticipation. The choice and conviction that life is worth living. Opposites: hopelessness, despair.

Trust: The decision to believe that another person is reliable and honest. Opposite: suspicion.

LOVE

Compassion: The decision to act to allay someone else's hurt or pain. Compassion is love in action.

Tolerance: The decision to suspend judgment and value others as worthy human beings. Tolerance may take faith.

Humility: The decision to accept all as interdependent and equal with none higher or lower than the rest.

Vs. Egoism: The decision expressed in words and deeds to value the thoughts and feelings of others as highly as one's own.

Vs. Apathy: The decision to express affectionate concern or devotion. Genuine love cannot be uninvolved.

Vs. Hostility: The decision to act with empathy, benevolence, fairness, goodness, kindness, and helpfulness.

*Permission granted to reproduce for classroom use. Taken from **Affective Self-Esteem** by Katherine Krefft, M.Ed., Ph.D. © 1993, Accelerated Development Inc., Publishers, 3808 W. Kilgore Avenue, Muncie, IN 47304-4896.*

UNIT VI:
CONCLUSION

CAMELOT

OBJECTIVES

Learners will demonstrate their comprehension of

1. the key concepts taught in Lessons One through Four as evidenced by class discussion in an oral review;

2. the impact of emotions and ignorance about emotions on society as illustrated by participation in a social studies analysis; and

3. the role of comfortable, positive emotions as shown by teacher-directed activities with Activity Sheets 19.1, 20.1, 20.2, and 21.1.

MATERIALS

- Magic Wand

- Chalkboard or overhead projector

- Social studies texts and other relevant books

- A synopsis of the story of Camelot

- Activity Sheets 19.1, 20.1, 20.2, and 21.1, "Peak Emotions"

- Journals for learners

CONTENT

1. **Review**

   Collect carryover assignment. Review the last lesson.

   - Why do we call invalid guilt the yuck blob?

   - How are the yuck blob and dark sorcerer related?

- Together what do they produce?

- Why is guilt a particularly human emotion?

- What is guilt?

- What self-talk defines an expectation?

- From where do expectations come?

- Describe valid, healthy guilt and its purpose.

- What does forgiveness have to do with guilt?

- What is the secret source of unhealthy guilt?

- Compare and contrast valid and invalid guilt.

- What does self-esteem have to do with guilt?

- What is Obsessive-compulsive Disorder?

- How may one destroy the yuck blob?

- Name three important things to do in Step C.

- How have you used what you have learned?

- Close your eyes. What is on the bulletin board?

2. **Review of Fundamentals**

a. **Review Emotions Versus Facts.**

Remind learners that we began by examining the difference between emotions and facts. Elicit the definitions in Lesson One and write them on the board.

Emotions =	**Facts =**

Review with learners the common misunderstandings about emotions. (See Lesson One.) Then, ask, *"How have your ideas about emotions changed as we've studied these lessons?"* As you pass the wand, go through each misunderstanding and list it on the board. Continue, *"This may be what you used to think. What do you think now?"* and *"What would you now tell someone who told you this?"* Continue to review Lessons One through Four.

b. **Describe How Emotions Are Like Water.**

Emotions and water both ebb and flow in a wavelike flux. The normal flow is up and down, on-off, ebb and flow. We may go with the flow or build dams. Emotions and water produce power, one produces emotional energy and the other, hydroelectricity. Both may be misdirected and misused as in a flood and in inappropriately and unacceptably expressed emotions.

c. **Identify Ways Emotions and Magic Are Alike.**

Both transform one thing into another. Both are not always what they appear. Both produce effects by unseen means and give special power. We have misunderstandings about both. Both are mysterious, fascinating, puzzling, and long hold our attention.

d. **Review Why We Tend to Dam Up Uncomfortable Emotions.**

To avoid pain. Because we are (or were!) ignorant of how to handle them constructively.

e. **Name The Most Challenging Human Emotions.**

Anger, fear, grief, and guilt.

f. **Review the Magic A, B, C's.**

A. Allow the emotion. Admit it.

B. Be with the emotion. Feel it.

C. Channel the emotion. Take constructive action.

g. **Identify Two Main Categories for Channeling Emotions and Give Examples.**

Verbal and nonverbal. See Lesson Three for examples.

h. **Define Self-talk.**

Thoughts. What you say to yourself in your head about yourself and your world.

i. **Explain Why We Call Thoughts Self-talk.**

To emphasize that we ourselves are responsible for our thoughts. To remind ourselves that we have the power to direct them.

j. **Name the Two Parts of Emotion.**

The feeling part and the thinking part.

k. **Describe the Thinking Part of Emotion.**

What one says to oneself about the emotion, the mental self-talk, the cognitive component.

l. **Describe the Feeling Part of Emotion.**

The physiological correlates and effects in the body. The release of hormones and other biochemical changes.

m. **Define Before Self-talk. Define After Self-talk.**

Before Self-talk is the secret self-talk, the magic words before feeling or not feeling the emotion. After Self-talk determines whether we stop or continue the emotion after the initial physiological discharge.

3. **Camelot**

Tell the tale of Camelot. Read a passage from the Tennyson classic, *Idylls of the King,*[7] play a selection of songs from the 1960 musical, *Camelot,* or give a dramatic rendition of the story of Arthur and the Table Round.

Explain, *"Camelot has timeless appeal because it is the story of how people not so very different from us confronted the challenging emotions of anger, fear, grief, guilt, and jealousy. In fact, it is the tale of how they **failed** to meet the challenge of those uncomfortable emotions. It is the saga of self-talk confused time and again by powerful emotions.*

"The King believed that his was the Rule of Reason. But in the end he lost his kingdom because neither he nor his Queen nor Lancelot—no, not even good Sir Galahad—knew very much at all about how to constructively channel and direct their emotions.

"BUT—the Prophecy says that Camelot will come again. Arthur is 'the once and future King.' In this lesson we shall take a look at what we all must do if Camelot is to come again—at what we must do to build a real Camelot, the best possible Camelot of all."

4. **The Impact of Emotions on Society**

Continue, *"In this lesson we'll look at how the twentieth century created the exact opposite of Camelot, Nazi Germany before and during World War II.*

---

[7] Tennyson, A.L. (1901). *Idylls of the king.* New York: Thomas Crowell Co. For the tale of Camelot, see also: Baines, M. (1962). *Sir Thomas Malory's Le Morte D'Arthur: A rendition in modern idiom.* New York: Bramhall House. Some relevant movies are *The Sword of Lancelot* (1963), *The Legend of King Arthur* (1974), and *Excalibur* (1981).

"We've seen that emotions are intrinsic and essential facets of our humanity. But ignorance about emotions is widespread and epidemic. We must magnify one person's lack of knowledge about emotions millions of times over to see the scope of it. No one is immune. What applies to the elementary school student applies as well to the leaders of nations. But a child's temper tantrum disturbs relatively few people. When the leader of a nation throws a temper tantrum, nations go to war.

"In society as in an individual only healthy emotions provide a check on the excesses and errors of so-called, invalid reason. **Invalid reason** *is reason distorted by anger, fear, grief, and guilt. Such 'reason' ends up quite unreasonable. In fact, it is not reason at all."*

Diagram the following on the board.

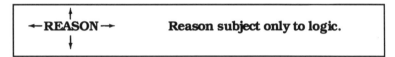

Draw arrows outward in four directions from the word, Reason. Explain that pure reason, true reason, is subject only to the premises of logic. The art of logic is so challenging it entertained philosophers for centuries.

But no one may **always** maintain a state of pure reason. We are emotional as well as reasonable creatures. We deny it. The very denial points to fear of emotions.

Thus, reason influenced by emotions uses self-talk to follow its own self-created premises to any conclusion desired. In short, invalid reason may talk itself into anything, even murder.

Draw a box at the outer edge of the arrows in the diagram. Around the outer perimeter write Emotion four times. Draw arrow tips pointing inward.

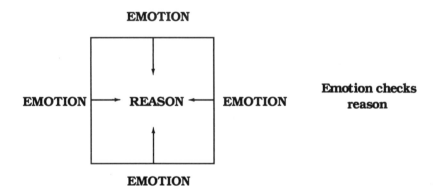

Passing the wand, elicit from learners emotions that check reason, particularly, anger, fear, grief, and guilt. Write each of these emotions next to one "Emotion" word.

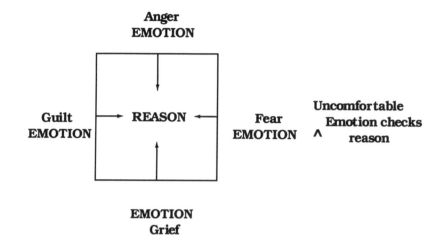

Explain, *"Reason tries to act reasonably but finds itself operating through a filter of emotion. When we do not know how to constructively handle emotions, they end up handling us! But we cannot admit that is what happened, so we invent self-talk that we pretend is reasonable."*

Stress to learners, *"Healthy emotions are a check on the excesses and errors of invalid reason. To see how this works, we are going to examine a major historical event of the twentieth century, Nazi Germany. We shall look at one singular, historical event to demonstrate what happens when garbage thinking prevails and invalid reason runs amuck."*

Leave the diagram on the board as you continue.

5. **When Camelot Was Not**

If necessary, circulate relevant social studies texts and other books about this era. However, the point is not to center on instruction about this crucial time of human history but to permit learners the opportunity to apply their new knowledge about emotions to an actual event. The discussion may be as narrow or as wide-ranging as time allows.

On the board list four columns.

Nazi Germany			
FEAR	**ANGER**	**GRIEF**	**GUILT**

Pass the wand as you lead the discussion with the following questions. As answers are given to the first questions, place large check marks under the columns of emotions that apply. With the remaining questions write key words or phrases under the proper columns.

- What is the ***primary*** emotion Hitler used? (Fear)

- What other emotions did he use? (Anger, grief, distorted guilt, shame, jealousy)

- Look at Hitler's face in old films and pictures. What emotions do you see there? (Primarily, anger. Often, unalloyed rage)

- Before World War II what did the Germans fear? (Relate response to Germany in the 1930's, e.g., fear of economic collapse, fear of continuing French retribution, etc. See any social studies text.)

- Before World War II did the German people have some cause for depression and grief? (Loss of territory, money, and national pride after World War I)

- What were Hitler and the Nazis angry about? How did they express that anger? (Germany's continuing losses and one-down position from World War I angered them. They expressed their anger in the key decisions of the Nazi regime, most notably in "the final solution" and in waging war.)

- The Nazis killed 16 million people. Why did they not feel guilty? (Relate to expectations. See Lesson Twenty. Let learners use their imaginations to guess at the extreme distortions in self-talk the Nazi elite used to absolve themselves from guilt.)

- Do you think the Magic A, B, C's would have helped Hitler? Pretend they would. Tell him how to apply them. (Accept various responses. Most likely, new information about emotions would have helped Hitler only when he was seven years old.)

- In the end Hitler committed suicide. What emotions does that demonstrate? (Explosive rage. Grief over the loss of his dreams and goals. Fear of the approaching Allies. Not guilt: he was unrepentant to the end.)

- Loss has two major emotional outcomes depending on how we choose to respond. What path did Germany choose? (The path of resentment and anger expressed as hostility.)

- What alternate path was possible but not followed? (The path of empathy leading to compassion and love.)

Then, conclude and summarize as follows.

- All these distorted emotions converted Nazi self-talk into monstrous garbage thinking. Describe what you think some of this self-talk was. Connect the proper emotional process with that self-talk.

Pass the wand to elicit answers similar to the these.

NOTES	Self-talk	Emotional Process
	We are the master race.	Compensation for fear
	We must rule the world.	Distortion of fear and anger
	Jews are inferior.	Projection of fear, prejudice
	We lost so much after WWI. We deserve to conquer all we can.	Distortion of grief and anger into resentment, revenge, and hostility as aggression
	We can do no wrong.	Denial of guilt
	It's okay to kill Jews.	Fear projected outward in anger as hatred and hostility.

Summarize, *"Nazi Germany is a prime example on the national level of misused, misdirected, denied, and projected emotions. A good Nazi would be the last to admit he was afraid of anything. Hitler was famous for his angry rages, but he believed he was a reasonable man. Not only that, many other people believed he had a reasonable plan for Germany, or they would not have followed him. Murder is not 'reasonable.' It is aggressively expressed anger, pure and simple.*

"Nazi Germany is a key example of the failure of human empathy. If you 'feel with' someone else's pain, you cannot persecute them or torture them or slaughter them in gas chambers."

Erase the words anger, fear, grief, and guilt from the diagram on the board. Replace them with the words empathy, compassion, charity, and love as follows.

COMPASSION

LOVE → REASON ← CHARITY

POSITIVE
Emotion checks
∧ reason

EMPATHY

Then, sum up the discussion of Nazi Germany. *"Given what Hitler wanted to do, Nazi Germany was a 'reasonable' state. It takes intelligence and reason logically applied to invent the most efficient means of mass murder. Nazi Germany did not happen because people were stupid, illogical, uneducated, and unreasoning. It happened because empathy as a constructive modulator of reason was discarded. Compassion was discarded."*

6. Conclusion

After weeks of study about uncomfortable emotions, a reasonable question a learner might raise is, *"What about the positive emotions?"* The comfortable, positive emotions of love, joy, excitement, and anticipation are Nature's way of making life worth living. They are Nature's most potent natural reinforcers.

However, handling these emotions is seldom, if ever, as challenging as handling the uncomfortable ones. Handling happiness is not like handling fear. It seems we need no one to tell us what to do to deal with joy.

We need anger management but not surprise management. Without instruction most people know how to enjoy a positive surprise. We do not repress joy the way we repress anger and fear. When it comes to comfortable emotions, we naturally express the A, B, C's. Normally, we allow, feel, and easily express the unchallenging emotions. That is why they are unchallenging and comfortable.

The comfortable emotions bring pleasure. Therefore, they are crucial elements of our lives. But we do not run from them. We seek them. They are not challenging in the same way as the uncomfortable, painful emotions.

Living a life that constructively addresses the full scope of emotional pain releases the full power of positive potential, also. There is no courage without fear. Determination feeds on anger, on just enough anger to move us to endure with tenacity. Righteous anger transforms nations and individuals for the good. Compassion and empathy proceed from grief. Healthy guilt drives us to our knees so that we may stand again as better human beings.

ACTIVITIES

Choose one or a combination. Assign one for carryover.

1. Summing Up

Direct learners to write a list of the ten most important things they shall remember from these 21 lessons.

2. Lists of Feeling Words Activities

Direct learners to invent an activity they may do by making use of any or all lists of feeling words. Retain their brilliant ideas for the next class you teach.

3. Passionate Peak Emotions
"Peak Emotions" (Activity Sheet 21.1)

Use the activity sheet as a starting point for discussion. Learners may enjoy writing a poem about one of the six peak emotions. The language teacher may direct that a particular form of poem, for example, a sonnet, be written. Budding poets may draw from the several lists of feelings for dynamic words that express the passion of emotion.

BULLETIN BOARD MATERIAL

1. Camelot is the kingdom of the Heart.

2. To love your life, live your love.

Name: _____   Date: _____

Activity Sheet 21.1
PEAK EMOTIONS

Constructive decisions do not always have comfortable emotions attached. Empathy for someone else's pain hurts. Faith may feel like a fog of darkness. Hope is often purely mental. Trust frequently feels very frightening. Love in action may be devoid of good, sweet feelings.

But on those rare and precious life moments when the thinking and feeling parts of emotion mesh with the **spiritual,** then the highest of human emotions are felt.

Six Peak Emotions	The Emotion Produces Feelings Of
Empathy	Whatever the other is feeling. Compassionate love.
Forgiveness	Peace. Relief. Release from hurt and anger.
Faith	Serenity. Absence of fear. Feeling safe and protected.
Hope	Enthusiasm. Eagerness. Pleasure of anticipation. Feeling a future joy in the present.
Trust	Confidence. Assurance. Confident expectation.
Love	Joy. Delight. Warmth. Interest. Attraction. Satisfaction. The pleasure of connection and union.

*Permission granted to reproduce for classroom use. Taken from **Affective Self-Esteem** by Katherine Krefft, M.Ed., Ph.D.* © 1993, Accelerated Development Inc., Publishers, 3808 W. Kilgore Avenue, Muncie, IN 47304-4896.

INDEX

INDEX

Thief
    sorcerer 156
Threats 78
    definition 62
    ego 73-5
    fairness 74, 80-1
    imagined 80
Trick
    sorcerer's anger 159
    word 85-90
Twain, M. xxvi, 138, 139
Type A
    personality 55

U

Unknown 112

V

Van Buren, A. 183

W

Wand
    See magic wand
    magic 3-9
    War on drugs xiv
Winfrey, O. 171
Wizard's boxes 77-84
Wizardry, words of 31-7
Word
    tricks 85-90
Words of wizardry 31-7

Katherine Krefft, M.Ed., Ph.D.

A clinical psychologist and educator, Dr. Katherine Krefft's particular area of expertise is affective education, a field that combines her more than twenty years' experience in education and psychology. In her workshops, lectures, and writings Dr. Krefft presents a positive view of our most challenging emotions—anger, fear, grief, and guilt—as applied to critical, current issues such as substance abuse prevention. A native of Louisiana, Dr. Krefft is a family therapist in private practice in southeastern Massachusetts.